International Dispute Settlement in an Evolving Global Society
Constitutionalization, Accessibility, Privatization

This book is the outcome of the Sir Hersch Lauterpacht Memorial Lectures delivered by the author at Cambridge University in 2001. It addresses three salient issues of contemporary international dispute settlement: the development of international constitutional law in a global society; the increasing access of the individual; and the developing role of international private arbitration.

The book discusses recent thoughts and proposals concerning a new role for the International Court of Justice in performing judicial constitutional functions, with particular reference to the United Nations and the trends toward the recognition of judicial review. It also addresses the question of the eventual establishment of an International Constitutional Court.

The increasing access of individuals to international dispute settlement is examined in the light of ICSID arbitration, free trade agreements and other developments in the WTO. Emerging trends in the organization of international commercial arbitration are discussed in the light of privatization arrangements.

FRANCISCO ORREGO VICUÑA is Professor of International Law at the Institute of International Studies and Law School, University of Chile. He is currently the President of the World Bank Administrative Tribunal and a member of the ICSID Panels of Conciliators and Arbitrators by appointment of the President of the World Bank. He has lectured in universities in the USA, Europe, the Pacific and South America, and at the Hague Academy of International Law.

International Dispute Settlement in an Evolving Global Society

Constitutionalization, Accessibility, Privatization

FRANCISCO ORREGO VICUÑA

Hersch Lauterpacht Memorial Lectures
2001

Lauterpacht Research Centre for International Law
University of Cambridge

CAMBRIDGE
UNIVERSITY PRESS

PUBLISHED BY THE PRESS SYNDICATE OF THE UNIVERSITY OF CAMBRIDGE
The Pitt Building, Trumpington Street, Cambridge, United Kingdom

CAMBRIDGE UNIVERSITY PRESS
The Edinburgh Building, Cambridge, CB2 2RU, UK
40 West 20th Street, New York, NY 10011–4211, USA
477 Williamstown Road, Port Melbourne, VIC 3207, Australia
Ruiz de Alarcón 13, 28014 Madrid, Spain
Dock House, The Waterfront, Cape Town 8001, South Africa

http://www.cambridge.org

First published 2004

Printed in the United Kingdom at the University Press, Cambridge

Typeface Monotype Baskerville 11/13 pt.   *System* LaTeX 2_ε [TB]

A catalogue record for this book is available from the British Library

ISBN 0 521 84239 5 hardback

Contents

Preface

I have been greatly honored by the invitation of Sir Elihu Lauterpacht and the Lauterpacht Research Centre for International Law at the University of Cambridge to deliver the Sir Hersch Lauterpacht Memorial Lectures for 2001. Because these are the first Lauterpacht Memorial Lectures at the beginning of a new century, it is appropriate to focus on a subject that is likely to endure for many years and to which Sir Hersch Lauterpacht greatly contributed in his own time.

The new arrangements for dispute settlement under international law in an evolving international society pose a number of key questions. First, it must be asked what are the likely characteristics of international society in the foreseeable future and what will be their impact upon the international legal order. The evolution that took place in this respect during the twentieth century offers a number of discernible trends that might serve to identify the basic features of the international society and of international law.

The second major question arises from the fact that international relations in an evolving society, one that is still developing its governing structure and rules, necessarily result in a whole set of new issues associated with the different types of disputes that need to be attended to in the changing legal environment. This in turn raises the question of the most adequate dispute settlement arrangements for handling the new legal, moral and political concerns of the international community.

Three central concerns of the international community will be explored in these lectures. First, the question of the need to establish and identify basic constitutional rules for the governance of international society will be discussed. In this context one might consider the feasibility of establishing an International Constitutional Court, as well as the role the International Court of Justice has had and is likely to have in dealing with constitutional issues. While this raises importantly the problem of the structure and pow-ers of the United Nations, it is not restricted to the ambit of any one organization; it also covers many questions of general international law.

The emergence of the individual as a subject and actor of international law is a second major concern to be explored. This aspect relates both to the models that are already available to settle disputes involving both state and individual interests and to the needs and developments that might be envisaged in this field. However, although considerable progress has been and is being made, some important limits have become evident; attending to these with care is necessary if we are to avoid a distortion of the true function of these new arrangements.

As international society becomes both more complex and interrelated the number of disputes likely to be submitted to international procedures is expected to grow exponentially; this is already evident from current prac-tice. The feasibility of establishing a structured or semi-structured mecha-nism of alternative dispute resolution at the international level will also be explored, particularly with a view to attend the many disputes that relate to transnational business and commercial activities.

The author had the opportunity and the privilege to participate as a co-rapporteur on the subject of dispute settlement for the Centennial Com-memoration of the First Peace Conference. This event took place in 1999 in The Hague and St. Petersburg, at the invitation of the Dutch and Russian governments, just as it had done a century earlier. During the work lead-ing to this commemoration and the discussions held on the subject, many ideas were contributed by distinguished international lawyers and judges, of which many have contributed to the present shape of these lectures.

It is hoped that this discussion will provoke new thoughts and eventually lead to new proposals on the improvement of current dispute settlement arrangements under international law, so as to facilitate the task of both present and future international courts and tribunals, and other institu-tions. This in itself would, of course, be the greatest homage to Sir Hersch Lauterpacht, whose vision of an international society under law had at its heart the need for just and effective international judicial institutions.

Acknowledgements

The author wishes to acknowledge the many useful suggestions made by colleagues and friends in the preparation and revision of these lectures. Particular mention must be made of Sir Elihu Lauterpacht, Professor James Crawford, Dr. Joanna Gomula and Mr. Darren Peacock, all from the Lauterpacht Research Centre for International Law at the University of Cambridge. Paz Zarate, from the Institute of International Studies of the University of Chile, also greatly helped in the organization of the tables and bibliography.

The research carried out in the preparation of these lectures was made possible under Grant No. 1000755 of the Chilean National Fund for Scientific and Technological Development on "New Alternatives for the Settlement of Disputes under International Law: trends for the twenty-first century" (2000–2002).

Abbreviations

APEC	Asia Pacific Economic Cooperation
ASEAN	Association of South East Nations
CSCE	Conference on Security and Co-operation in Europe
DSU	WTO Dispute Settlement Understanding
ECJ	Court of Justice of the European Community
ECR	European Communities Court of Justice Reports
EU	European Union
FAO	Food and Agricultural Organization
GATS	General Agreement on Trade and Services
GATT	General Agreement on Tariffs and Trade
IBRD	International Bank for Reconstruction and Development
ICC	International Criminal Court
ICJ	International Court of Justice
ICSID	International Centre for the Settlement of Investment Disputes
ICTY	International Criminal Tribunal for the Former Yugoslavia
IDI	Institut de Droit International
ILA	International Law Association
ILC	International Law Commission
IMF	International Monetary Fund
MERCOSUR	Southern Cone Common Market
NAFTA	North American Free Trade Agreement
OECD	Organization for Economic Co-operation and Development
OSCE	Organization for Security and Co-operation in Europe
PCA	Permanent Court of Arbitration

List of abbreviations

PCIJ	Permanent Court of International Justice
RIAA	Reports of International Arbitral Awards
UN	United Nations
UNCC	United Nations Compensation Commission
UNCITRAL	United Nations Commission on International Trade Law
UNTS	United Nations Treaties Series
WIPO	World Intellectual Property Organization
WTO	World Trade Organization

Table of treaties

Table of cases

1

An evolving international society: institutionalization, privatization, globalization

The changes in international society during the twentieth century have clearly established a pattern of evolution from the traditional forms of inter-state relations to an increasingly institutionalized community of nations.[1] Hedley Bull identified five main features of international society as being characteristic of the Grotian tradition: the central place of natural law; the universality of international society; the role of individuals and non-state groups in such society; solidarism in the enforcement of rules; and the absence of international institutions.[2] A number of these features are still shaping modern international society, thus providing a background of continuity to the changes taking place, changes which will now be reviewed.

Increasing institutionalization

Many changes have intervened in the organization of international society in the last few decades, while various aspects of the traditional arrangements continue to influence the shaping of this evolution. It should be noted first that, irrespective of past doctrinal discussions about natural and positive law, it is a fact that most contemporary developments are inspired by the need to ensure human freedom, dignity and welfare, aims inextricably related to our shared humanity. It is next apparent that international society adheres to the ideal of universality, despite powerful recent trends towards regionalism.[3]

[1] Hedley Bull, Benedict Kingsbury and Adam Roberts (eds.), *Hugo Grotius and International Relations* (1992).
[2] Hedley Bull, "The importance of Grotius in the study of international relations" in Bull, *Hugo Grotius*, pp. 65–93, 78–91.
[3] W.W. Rostow: "The coming age of regionalism. A 'metaphor' for our time?," *Encounter* (June 1990) 3–7.

1

Although this has prompted occasional tensions and competition between centralized international action and the role of regional organizations, universality and regionalism are generally complementary features of international society. Third, the role of individuals and non-state actors in the international system has become significant, threatening at times to curtail the exclusive role of the state.[4] However, in the light of occasional excesses concerning the role of such non-state actors, the limits and conditions for the participation of non-governmental organizations in the work of international society and the making of international law have been reaffirmed from time to time.

In terms of the arrangements for collective security, solidarism in the enforcement of the law and in the repression of threats to international peace and security has continued to be the dominant feature. But there have been significant innovations in the enforcement of other more specialized arrangements, especially in the fields of trade and the environment. A major change that must be noted, by contrast with the absence or limited role of international institutions in the past, is the powerful life of international organizations,[5] perhaps less evident in the political sphere but significant in other major areas of international cooperation. However, even in this context the delegation of powers to international organizations, and still more any eventual transfer of competences, remains under the close control of states.[6]

The emergence of a multi-centric and multi-cultural international society is another significant aspect of the intervening changes in international life.[7] Political and economic power is, of course, a predominant element in the working of international society, but some aspects of it are becoming increasingly decentralized and need to take into account other influential factors. While some elements of this power structure, such as military capability and political influence, have occasionally shown a trend towards a unipolar system, and to that extent have also adversely affected diversity in the governing of the international society, these features do not seem likely to prevail in the long run.

[4] Societé Française pour le Droit International, *L'État souverain à l'aube du XXIe siècle* (Colloque de Nancy, 1994).

[5] Louis B. Sohn, "The role of international law in the 21st century," address at the Vrije Universiteit, Brussels, 23 March 1990, 5–6.

[6] Eileen Denza, "Two legal orders: divergent or convergent?" 48 *International and Comparative Law Quarterly* (1999) 257–284, at 259.

[7] Edith Brown Weiss, "The new international legal system" in *Perspectives on International Law* (1995), pp. 63–82, at 66.

While for the reasons given, international society has been deeply transformed as compared with the past, it nonetheless evidences a *continuum* that should not be disregarded in evaluating the meaning and extent of current trends and their implications for the future.

In this context, some current utopian theories, while academically challenging, do not appear to reflect the realism necessary to make them feasible in the foreseeable future. The continuing absence of war among democracies,[8] the obsolescence of conflict[9] or the arrogant view that history has come to an end with the undisputed prevalence of liberal-democratic principles[10] are among some of the announcements greeting the new century. But, from the point of view of evolution of international society, they are not less utopian than the prospects for a world government. The rise and fall of Great Powers[11] or the collapse of empires,[12] have also attracted much attention in the context of current transformations. However, these views, inspired by individual readings of the historical evidence, may not necessarily be reflected in the design of the society of the future.

A developing process of globalization and its limits

As international society evolves, the phenomenon of globalization is taking hold. Beginning with the integration of financial markets and followed by the partial liberalization of world trade, globalization appears to be a lasting feature of international society. These developments are in turn linked to the revolution in communications and information technology, the fourth technological revolution,[13] new horizons in science, and the powerful emergence of leading developing economies that have introduced new dimensions into international competitiveness. The success and expansion of market economies are at the very heart of the process of globalization,

---

[8] Dean V. Babst, "A force for peace" 14 *Industrial Research* (1972) 55–58; R.J. Rummel, "Libertarianism and international violence" 27 *Journal of Conflict Resolution* (1983) 27–71; Bruce Russett, "The politics of an alternative security system: toward a more democratic and therefore more peaceful world" in Burns Weston (ed.), *Alternatives to Nuclear Deterrence* (1989).

[9] John Mueller, *Retreat from Doomsday: The Obsolescence of Major War* (1989).

[10] Francis Fukuyama, "The end of history?" 16 *The National Interest* (Summer 1989) 3–18.

[11] Paul Kennedy, *The Rise and Fall of Great Powers* (1987).

[12] Hugh Trevor-Roper and George Urban, "Aftermaths of Empire: the lessons of upheavals and destabilisation," *Encounter* (December 1989) 3–16.

[13] Rostow, "The coming age," 3.

and have a specific influence on the organizational needs of international society and its legal institutions.[14]

Notwithstanding integration that results from globalization, there is also the simultaneous trend of decentralization. Both in economic and political terms, international society is becoming increasingly decentralized. The ignition of regional self-contained conflicts, the painful consultations many times required to achieve a consensus on the appropriate action by major political powers, or the semi-autonomous operation of international markets are all indications of such a phenomenon. Similarly, the diffusion of economic power and the prospective emergence of alternative centers of political power, the resurgence of religious influences in the conduct of both domestic and international affairs, the affirmation of cultural values, and outbursts of nationalism, are clear indications that globalization is conducive not only to centralization but to decentralization as well. In fact, the two trends appear to be complementary rather than contradictory. It also appears that globalization is not as global as it is often thought but relates to specific fields of activity that states and other entities undertake at an international or even national level.

As Judge Rosalyn Higgins has aptly explained, globalization and other concurrent developments have affected the traditional notion of a sovereign state in a myriad of ways.[15] Besides business and finance, also governance, human rights and environmental protection have a significant impact upon the powers of traditional sovereignty. Notwithstanding the extent of this phenomenon, the state is likely to remain a central actor in the international system. There is currently a reaction to reaffirm sovereignty in some key aspects of social life where it is perceived that contrary trends have gone too far. While this reaction is more apparent in the case of developing countries, it may also be detected in the developed world and in the functioning of important organizations such as the European Union and other integration mechanisms.[16]

The view that disorder and chaos prevail in the international system[17] is not mistaken insofar as conflict and confrontation, current or potential, are still very much in existence and will not disappear. However, just as

---

[14] See David Held and Anthony McGrew, *Globalization and Anti-Globalization* (2002); David Held (ed.), *A Globalizing World?: Culture, Economics, Politics* (2000); Jürgen Basedow and Toshiyuki Kono (eds.), *Legal Aspects of Globalization: Conflict of Laws, Internet, Capital Markets and Insolvency in a Global Economy* (2000).

[15] Rosalyn Higgins, "International law in a changing international system" 58 *Cambridge Law Journal* (1999) 78–95, at 82–84.

[16] Denza, "Two legal orders," 269–273.   [17] Higgins, "International law," 81.

scientific theory may find order in chaos, so too is the international system not altogether deprived of rules and institutions that increasingly point towards an organized conduct of international affairs. Among such institutions, dispute settlement arrangements are called to play a particularly active role in securing order in the international system.

Changing character of international law

The changes that have taken place in international society have naturally influenced international law and its current features. Again, however, conflicting views exist on the extent of the transformation of the international legal system. Some scholars believe that this system of law is and will remain horizontal in character, governing in essence an inter-state society.[18] Others stress the growing introduction of vertical features where the rule of law applies, to some extent at least, over and above the role of states.[19]

The reality appears to be somewhere in between. Because changes in international society tend to affirm the prevalence of human values, there are areas of the law that take the shape of a vertical structure. To some degree, this vertical structure subjects states and other actors of the international system to a rule of law that develops independently from their express consent. But this "verticality" is still the exception, not the general rule. It also poses extremely difficult questions as to who should determine the applicable rules, and raises concerns about legitimacy, transparency and democratic guarantees. Above all, it raises the question whether it responds to a genuine process under international law or simply to the political power and influence of given states or groups of interests, more or less accidental or transitory.

Within this overall framework it is possible to realize that, as Wolfang Friedmann had anticipated,[20] international law has developed from a structure of coordination to one of cooperation. In the latter, the attainment of common goals is more actively pursued. This evolution may, however, lead to certain forms of subordination within the legal system. The existence of rules or of obligations described as *jus cogens* or *erga omnes* responds, to some

---

[18] Prosper Weil, "Le droit international en quête de son identité", Cours Général de Droit International Public, 237 VI *Académie de Droit International* (1992–VI) 13–369, at 33, 87–88.

[19] C.M. Chinkin, "The challenge of soft law: development and change in international law" 38 *International and Comparative Law Quarterly* (1989) 850–866; Geoffrey Palmer, "New ways to make international environmental law" 86 *American Journal of International Law* (1992) 259–283.

[20] Wolfang Friedmann, *The Changing Structure of International Law* (1964).

degree, to the identification of forms of normative subordination, but on many occasions these distinctions are more a matter of academic interest than of practical significance. The same might be said of the earlier efforts of the International Law Commission to introduce the concept of crimes of states under international law, later abandoned.[21] The vertical structure of international law has found more prominent expression in the experience of the European Community. Its legal system is based on a body of law enacted under the basic treaties that can be directly applied in Member States, while its implementation is subject to mechanisms of administrative and judicial control, extending even to penalties and other forms of enforcement.[22]

Integrating the fragmented structure of the legal system

The vast normative expansion experienced in international law, coupled with the changing role of the sources of international law and with efforts to identify such new sources,[23] has resulted in a growing uncertainty about which law is applicable to given issues or activities. A major challenge is to ascertain the consent of states in respect of those rules, particularly in the context of the work of international organizations and the adoption of "soft law" approaches.

The codification of international law in the course of multilateral treaty-making conferences has provided the opportunity to both clarify and develop the law, and to establish the limits of the states' consent. But, as Judge Higgins remarked, this effort is now a matter largely of the past, except for a few areas relating to the environment, arms control and bioethics.[24] The uncertainty about the state of international law cannot be eliminated by selective codification of specific topics, and may even deepen in future, particularly insofar as the greatest emphasis will be on the implementation of the law, taking into account its inter-temporal and inter-generational dimensions.[25]

The identification of the basic principles of international law has become a renewed priority. These principles should hold the normative structure together in an integrated manner, avoiding the negative effects of

---

[21] See now ILC Articles on Responsibility of States for Internationally Wrongful Acts, annexed to UNGA Resolution 56/83, 12 December 2001.
[22] Denza, "Two legal orders," 266–269.
[23] Oscar Schachter, *International Law in Theory and Practice* (1991), p. 10.
[24] Higgins, "International law," 79.
[25] Brown Weiss, "New international legal system," 77–79.

the dispersion of international law in a decentralized society and allowing for a coherent interpretation of the law. Because of the fragmentation of law-making bodies in the international community, the task of identifying central principles has become more urgent, particularly in order to allow the systematic examination of state practice and international legislation. The emergence of key constitutional rules in the international community and some of its major organizations, and the role of dispute settlement in this context, will be discussed in chapter 2.

This identification of key principles of international law must rely on the broad participation of states and their express consent, so as to ensure both the universality and the sustainability of the rules. Law-making majorities may be useful in the context of particular international negotiations and in the working of certain organizations, but they cannot substitute for the consensus of states. Still less can they result in the imposition of views that are not shared by the international community in general.

Transforming international law: developments and limitations

Although international law has kept with some of its traditional features it is also possible to identify a number of important innovations and transformations. First, states have accepted gradually to limit their sovereignty for the benefit of international organizations and the role of individuals, while keeping this process under strict control and restricting it to certain selected fields of activity only.

Second and as a result of this process, the gradual transfer of powers to international organizations is controlled and limited. Such organizations do not generally enjoy any autonomous law-making function and certainly do not, as a rule, assume authority above the state.

Third, the transfer of competences to international organizations, resulting in the renunciation of state sovereignty in particular areas of activity, is an exception in contemporary international law. It is a phenomenon more or less unique to the European Community and even in this case is subject to certain qualifications.[26] The limited experience available elsewhere has shown that this approach is constrained in its scope and is unlikely to be adopted more generally.

Fourth, the implementation of international law has been gradually subject to improvement by means of treaty and other arrangements which are

---

[26] Denza, "Two legal orders," 269–273.

conducive to a faster entry into force and eventually to the direct application of international rules at the domestic level. It is also coupled with mechanisms of verification and control, and occasionally the intervention of judicial bodies.[27] The lack of autonomous enforcement mechanisms and its dependence on state cooperation have thus seen some limited remedy.

Fifth, international law-making is increasingly becoming more transparent and subject to public scrutiny, prompting a more active participation of national Parliaments and public opinion.[28] The use of referendums in international legal and political matters, the examination of international negotiations by congressional bodies and the role of organized interest groups in the outcome of law-making is evidencing a changing trend in this area.

Sixth, domestic courts are increasingly resorting to the direct application of international law, both treaties and customary rules, prompting the need for some kind of international supervision to prevent misguided or abusive interpretations.

Preservation of national autonomy

International law will no doubt evolve as international society keeps changing, a process that must be perceived by states and public opinion not as antagonistic to legitimate expectations of national values and historic and cultural traditions, but rather as complementary to national autonomy. Progress in the international legal system will be jeopardized if it is perceived as working against the legitimate interests of national communities or if surreptitious methods are used to circumvent the legitimate objectives of its main actors and subjects, the states.

The preservation of democratic institutions and solutions is another fundamental reason why the international system must perform functions complementary to the national order. If the expression of political will in democratic societies aims at the establishment of certain values, models or solutions, it should not be negatively affected by the recourse to an international system that might be influenced by different values and interests, not supported by the state. This would probably result in the distortion of public decisions. Therefore, a new need arises for national societies to exercise democratic control over international law-making, its interpretation and implementation.

---

[27] Brown Weiss, "New international legal system," 73–74.
[28] Denza, "Two legal orders," 273–277.

The developments and interrelations discussed above pose a myriad of problems and challenges for the role of dispute settlement mechanisms in the international community. The problem is compounded because the purpose of these mechanisms is to decide upon conflicting views and inter-pretations relating to a legal system that is far from well settled and pre-dictable. The stability of the international legal system and the relationship with its constitutive elements thus depends heavily on the effectiveness of dispute settlement arrangements, formal and informal.

2

A constitutional court for an international society?

The process of decentralization of international society and international law makes it necessary to consider a new role for the basic principles of international law governing the international society. This element could enable a minimum degree of integration and coherence in such society and its legal order. In this context, the identification and development of such principles becomes a constitutional function.

This chapter will examine the main aspects of a long-standing constitutional debate relating to international law, with emphasis on its implications for the United Nations and the Security Council. The prospects for the establishment of a Constitutional Court for the world community, taking into account the role of the International Court of Justice, will also be examined.

Constitutional approaches to international law

The idea of introducing a constitutional dimension in international law is not new.[1] In 1926 Verdross discussed the notion of constitutional international law.[2] It was first identified with norms dealing with the structure, subdivision and distribution of spheres of jurisdiction in the international community,[3] and later associated with the most important rules of general

---

[1] For an historical account and present developments see generally Bardo Fassbender, "The United Nations Charter as constitution of the international community" 36 *Columbia Journal of Transnational Law* (1998) 529–619. See also generally Bardo Fassbender, *The UN Security Council Reform and the Right of Veto: A Constitutional Perspective* (1997).

[2] A. Verdross, *Die Verfassung der Völkerrechtsgemeinschaft* (1926).

[3] *Ibid.*, p. v, and see the discussion by Fassbender, "The United Nations Charter," 541–544.

international law[4] or specifically with the Principles embodied in the Charter of the United Nations.[5]

This evolution reflects both a procedural (or formal) approach and a substantive one.[6] It was owing to Kelsen's theoretical framework of the unity of the legal order and the identification of the basic norm of the international legal order as the ultimate reason for the validity of both the international and the national legal orders[7] that this constitutional approach became possible. This was, of course, also the theoretical basis of the pyramidal structure determining the primacy of international over national law.[8]

George Scelle also explored the theory of a constitutional international law. He referred to the norms that regulate the three important social functions of legislating, adjudicating and sanctioning,[9] and in this context dealt with the question of a hierarchy of norms in the international legal system.[10] His famous concept of states performing a "dédoublement fonctionnel"[11] was also related to this constitutional view. The "théorie de l'institution" elaborated by Hauriou contrasted an ordinary contract with a lasting institution created for the accomplishment of a social goal,[12] a concept subsequently applied by other authors to international institutions and their association with a constitution aiming at the "bien commun de l'humanité."[13]

---

[4] A. Verdross, *Völkerrecht* (2nd edn., 1950), p. 74. See also generally Hersch Lauterpacht, *The Function of Law in the International Community* (1933).

[5] A. Verdross, *Völkerrecht* (5th edn., 1964), p. 136. See also Alfred Verdross and Bruno Simma, *Universelles Völkerrecht: Theorie und Praxis* (1976), p. 5, and discussion by Fassbender, "The United Nations Charter," 541–542.

[6] Eric Suy, "The constitutional character of constituent treaties of international organizations and the hierarchy of norms" in *Recht Zwischen Umbruch und Bewahrung, Festschrift für Rudolf Bernhardt* (1995), pp. 267–277, at 268–269.

[7] Ian Brownlie, "International law at the fiftieth anniversary of the United Nations" 255 *Recueil des Cours de l'Academie de Droit International* (1995) 13–227, at 26–27.

[8] Suy, "Constitutional character," 269–270.

[9] G. Scelle, "Le droit constitutionnel international" in *Mélanges R. Carré de Malberg* (1933), pp. 503, at 514–515, and discussion by Suy, "Constitutional character," 268, 271–272.

[10] G. Scelle, *Précis de Droit des Gens*, Tome II (1934), pp. 410–411.

[11] See the discussion by Gaetano Arangio-Ruiz, "The normative role of the General Assembly of the United Nations and the Declaration of Principles of Friendly Relations" III *Recueil des Cours de l'Academie de Droit International* (1972) 635–636.

[12] M. Hauriou, "La théorie de l'institution et de la fondation. Essai de vitalisme social" 4 *La Cité Moderne et les Transformations du Droit*, Cahiers de la Nouvelle Journée (1925) 1, at 11, and discussion by Suy, "Constitutional character," 274–275.

[13] G. Renard, "Les bases philosophiques du droit international et la doctrine du 'Bien commun'" in *Archives de Philosophie du Droit* (1931), p. 465, at 476–477; A. Mestre, "Les traités et le droit interne" 42 IV *Recueil des Cours de l'Academie de Droit International* (1931) 233, at 301, and discussion by Suy, "Constitutional character," 275–276.

It is interesting to note that it was Georg Schwarzenberger who first developed a theory of a constitutional international law without the requirement of having a formal constitution in place.[14] Inspired by the English common law and the lack of a formal British constitution, he identified constitutional law with public law and policy, the concept of *public order*, on which the legal system is based. Because such public order cannot be modified by individual parties, the pertinent rules are *jus cogens*.[15] A similar approach, relying more on procedural aspects, was later developed by Jenks.[16]

A more intricate conceptual framework was adopted by the New Haven School.[17] In essence, it looks for a "constitutive process" of authoritative power providing for an institutional framework which will allocate indispensable functions and result in the adoption of "constitutive decisions" necessary for the making and administering of general community policy. While rejecting a normative approach and relying on policy-oriented formulations,[18] the constitutive process is nonetheless presented as conducive to the orderly governance of the social process of the world community under the rule of law.

Perhaps the most significant contemporary contribution to the constitutional approach to international law has been made by Hermann Mosler.[19] He does not go so far as to suggest that the international community is presently governed by a constitution, but rather identifies a number of constitutional elements with a restricted objective.[20] Mosler notes that even in earlier times, when no organization existed, international society was governed by a constitutional element that required consensus for the making of international law.[21]

As international society develops, the public order of the international community begins to take shape and some of its aspects become *jus cogens*.[22]

---

[14] G. Schwarzenberger, *International Law as Applied by International Courts and Tribunals*, vol. III, *International Constitutional Law* (1976), pp. 116–117, and discussion by Suy, "Constitutional character," 272–273.

[15] Schwarzenberger, *International Law*, p. 125.

[16] C.W. Jenks, *The Common Law of Mankind* (1958), p. 23, and discussion by Suy, "Constitutional character," 273–274.

[17] Myres S. McDougal *et al.*, "The world constitutive process of authoritative decision" in Myres S. McDougal and W. Michael Reisman, *International Law Essays: A Supplement to International Law in Contemporary Perspective* (1981), p. 191, at 192, and discussion by Fassbender, "The United Nations Charter," 544–546. See also the discussion by Brownlie, "International law," 27–29, and by Nicholas Onuf, "The constitution of international society" 5 *European Journal of International Law* (1994) 5, s. III.

[18] Brownlie, "International law," 28.

[19] Hermann Mosler, "The international society as a legal community", IV *Recueil des Cours de l'Academie de Droit International* (1974), 1–320.

[20] *Ibid.*, 32.   [21] *Ibid.*, 32.   [22] *Ibid.*, 33–36.

Political doctrines and international law principles still coexist in defining the general policy that governs the international community.[23] An important consequence of this approach is that it views the international community as being in a period of transition, evolving from a state where legal relations are purely of an horizontal nature into one with some elements of verticality and subordination.[24]

A less doctrinal and more pragmatic approach is represented by Philip Allott. It is difficult not to agree with his distinction between the legal constitution, the real constitution and the ideal constitution.[25] The first concerns the distribution and limits of social power, as well as its implementation and enforcement. The real constitution reflects the current realities of the social process, while the ideal constitution establishes our own model of desired society.

It is still more difficult not to agree that principles such as those described by Allott (transformation, delegation of power, intrinsic limitation of power, the supremacy of law, the supremacy of the social interest and social responsibility) have a constitutional dimension and are essential for the integration of the law.[26] One way or the other, the international community is developing and organizing these principles. But it is necessary to do so in a more self-aware and reflective way. As Allott remarks: "[f]ailing to recognize itself as a society, international society has not known that it has a constitution. Not knowing its own constitution, it has ignored the generic principles of a constitution."[27]

Constitutional debate in the context of the United Nations

The views outlined above were largely expressed from the perspective of legal reasoning and jurisprudential reflection. The next step is to extend those considerations to the examination of the United Nations Charter in a constitutional dimension. In so doing, however, a number of elements of a political character are brought into play, igniting a debate that straddles legal and political considerations and offers fewer possibilities of reaching any consensus or common point of view. Indeed, this debate raises serious questions relating to the nature of international law and to the legitimacy of particular arrangements for wielding power at the international level.

---

[23] *Ibid.*, 37–44.   [24] *Ibid.*, 31.
[25] Philip Allott, *Eunomia: A New Order for a New World* (1990), pp. 135–136, and discussion by Fassbender, "The United Nations Charter," 536.
[26] Allott, *Eunomia*, pp. 167–168.
[27] *Ibid.*, p. 418, as cited by Fassbender, "The United Nations Charter," 531.

Starting from the premise that the Conference of San Francisco was a "constitutional moment" in international law,[28] authors have looked for various constitutional features in the Charter of the United Nations. These range from the system of governance, providing for a legislature, an executive and a judiciary, however imperfect they may be,[29] to a normative hierarchy reflected in Article 103 of the Charter.[30] They include a number of other provisions relating to membership and amendment.[31] There can be no doubt that the Charter embodies a number of innovative provisions both in the material sense and in the organic or institutional sense.[32] The meaning and real effect of these provisions, however, lies at the very heart of the contemporary debate on the United Nations.

One school of thought sees in the constitutional features of the United Nations the opportunity for developing the ground rules that determine and allocate the functions needed to keep a political system on course, and particularly to reconcile conflicting freedoms and legitimate priorities.[33] This is often thought to imply that a system exclusively based on the juxtaposition of sovereign entities will not prove workable in the long run. It is therefore suggested that it should be the task of the United Nations to provide for an overarching or supporting structure that will bind the different elements of the international community.[34] The identification of values shared by the international community and the development of an organizational structure suitable for carrying out these functions and transcending the capacities of individual nations, are from this point of view some of the main contributions of the United Nations.[35]

---

[28] Fassbender, "The United Nations Charter," 573.

[29] Christian Tomuschat, "International law as the constitution of mankind" in United Nations, *International Law on the Eve of the Twenty-first Century* (1997), pp. 37–50, at 38, 44–48.

[30] See generally Suy, "Constitutional character."

[31] Fassbender, "The United Nations Charter," 576–580.

[32] Pierre-Marie Dupuy, "The constitutional dimension of the Charter of the United Nations revisited" 1 *Max Planck Yearbook of United Nations Law* (1997) 1–33, at 3. See also James Crawford, "The Charter of the United Nations as a constitution" in Hazel Fox (ed.), *The Changing Constitution of the United Nations* (1997), pp. 3–16; R. St. J. Macdonald, "The United Nations Charter: constitution or contract?" in R. St. J. Macdonald and Douglas M. Johnston (eds.), *The Structure and Process of International Law* (1983), pp. 889–912; R. St. J. Macdonald, "The Charter of the United Nations and the development of fundamental principles of international law" in Bin Cheng and E.D. Brown (eds.), *Contemporary Problems of International Law* (1988), pp. 196–215.

[33] Tomuschat, "Constitution of mankind," 38. On the development of democracy and international law see also J. Crawford, "Democracy and international law," *British Year Book of International Law* (1993) 123.

[34] Tomuschat, "Constitution of mankind," 43.   [35] *Ibid.*, 43.

This idealistic view of the world community entails two assumptions. The first is that international law has become, or is becoming, a vertical normative structure within which the autonomy of states is diluted, with the United Nations playing a central role in this development. The second assumption is that the United Nations has the legitimacy to undertake this constitutional task, both under the express terms of the Charter and by means of its broad interpretation, as is appropriate with respect to a constitutional instrument.[36]

These assumptions rely, it is argued, not so much on legal considerations but on political realities. It is thus maintained that a universal framework for action, or the constitution of mankind, cannot be directly related to individual human beings as such. Rather, the existing power centers must be relied upon.[37] In this context, it is thought that the privileges of the five permanent members of the Security Council have been granted not as an individual entitlement in recognition of a factual position of power but as a competence to be exercised in the interest of the international community in terms of a public trust.[38]

Other supporters of *realpolitik* believe more bluntly that the Charter is not a constitution and does not create a system concerned with the rule of law, but that the system is akin to that of a police state governed by the Security Council which is, and must be, a "law unto itself."[39]

These assumptions have been opposed by a different school of thought that relies on the traditional characteristics of international law and its horizontal nature.[40] First, it is believed that a "federalist" approach to the law of nations finds no justification in practice and is likely to be detrimental to the cause it promotes.[41] States have never accepted to become subdivisions of a larger universal entity.[42] Second, it is argued that nothing in the Charter of the United Nations can be held to have the implications for the organization of an international community and the diminution of the sovereignty of states that some authors are trying to read into it.

In this context, it is further argued, the only fundamental constitutional rule of international law is the equality of states and their exemption from

---

[36] For a discussion of the assumption relating to the constitutional interpretation of treaties, see Suy, "Constitutional character," 267.

[37] Tomuschat, "Constitution of mankind," 40.   [38] *Ibid.*, 47.

[39] For a discussion of these views see José E. Alvarez, "Judging the Security Council" 90 *American Journal of International Law* (1996) 1–39, at 1–2.

[40] Gaetano Arangio-Ruiz, "The 'federal analogy' and UN Charter interpretation: a crucial issue" 8 *European Journal of International Law* (1997) 1–28, at 26.

[41] Arangio-Ruiz, "Normative role," 624–625.

[42] Arangio-Ruiz, "The 'federal analogy,'" 14.

superior authority.[43] In respect of the role of the organs of the United Nations, it is believed that they are neither the legal representatives of a community composed of peoples or states, nor do they share international governmental functions with states.[44] It follows that no principle of constitutional interpretation can be accepted, still less the doctrine of implied powers,[45] and that political hegemony can be no source of legitimacy in international law.[46]

The debate surrounding the United Nations has extended into the realm of general international law. A rule stated by the Charter may be at the same time a norm of customary international law, whether because it was already part of customary international law before being embodied in the Charter or because it has come to be accepted as such.[47] Some Charter rules have a nexus with rules of *jus cogens* and *erga omnes* obligations, albeit not a necessary or automatic one.[48] In any event, there is a tendency to consider that treaty or customary norms which constitute the development of the basic principles and rules of the Charter may have a certain "constitutional" rank.[49]

This in turn has prompted a critical reaction about the extent of the legislative powers of the General Assembly, as for example in the context of the Declaration on Friendly Relations in 1970.[50] A similar reaction relates to the perceived use and abuse of customary international law to justify developments that would not be acceptable to states.[51]

This discussion is not unique to the United Nations; it concerns other major international organizations, with varying degrees of intensity. Within the European Communities a trend is emerging to limit the power of Member States to amend the constitutive treaties,[52] just as in some domestic constitutional systems there are certain categories of non-amendable principles.[53] However, the closely knit relationship that has been built

---

[43] Arangio-Ruiz, "Normative role," 665.   [44] *Ibid.*, 680.

[45] On the doctrine of implied powers in the United Nations see generally Arangio-Ruiz, "The 'federal analogy.'"

[46] *Ibid.*, 20–22.   [47] Dupuy, "Constitutional dimension," 7–11.

[48] *Ibid.*, 8–11. See also Fassbender, "The United Nations Charter," 589–593.

[49] Fassbender, "The United Nations Charter," 588.

[50] United Nations General Assembly, *Declaration on Principles of International Law Concerning Friendly Relations and Co-operation Among States*, UNGA Res. 2625 (XXV), 24 October 1970, GAOR XXV, Suppl. 28, at 121. See also generally Arangio-Ruiz, "Normative role."

[51] Arangio-Ruiz, "The 'federal analogy,'" 25–26.

[52] Fassbender, "The United Nations Charter," 603.

[53] See, e.g., Art. 79, para. 3, of the 1949 German Constitution and the comments on this and other texts by Fassbender, "The United Nations Charter," 602–603.

within the Community, and the commonly shared values, makes it so far a unique experience that bears no resemblance to international organizations of universal membership. Moreover, even in this case there is some reconsideration as to the nature of the arrangements and the powers of Member States, a reconsideration that will tend more towards a Europe of nations rather than to a federal system embodied in a constitution.[54]

This debate has to be linked to the discussion about the nature of international law outlined in chapter 1. No one doubts that international law seeks a balance between freedom of action by states and the interests of the community, however this community may be defined.[55] To that extent, some elements of verticality have been introduced and accepted in the international legal order, but this has been done with the consent and participation of states.

The legal order of the international community continues to be of a horizontal nature. However, as a result of idealistic or political intentions, attempts may sometimes be made to circumvent the will of states and to introduce into the international legal order interpretations or developments that are not genuinely the outcome of consensus. The legitimacy of such developments is then tainted.[56]

Judge Alvarez wrote that constitutions "can be compared to ships which leave the yards in which they have been built, and sail away independently, no longer attached to the dockyard."[57] True as this may be, the ship will always be bound by the design of its architect and the features assigned by its engineers. It will sail independently, but cannot transform itself into a different ship unless it is redesigned. The problem of international law at present is not with the kind of interpretation that allows for it to evolve independently but still within the bounds of its design. It is rather with those interpretations that seek to transform the law into what is desired by one interested viewpoint but that do not necessarily respond to the will

---

[54] See generally Eileen Denza, "Two legal orders: divergent or convergent?" 48 *International and Comparative Law Quarterly* (1999) 257–284. On the current political debate in Europe see "The triumph of nations" in *The Economist: The World in 2001* (2001), pp. 42–43.

[55] Christian Tomuschat, "Obligations arising for states without or against their will" 241 IV *Recueil des Cours de l'Academie de Droit International* (1993) 195, at 292, and discussion by Fassbender, "The United Nations Charter," 582.

[56] Georges Abi Saab, "'Humanité' et 'communauté internationale' dans la dialectique du droit international" in *Humanité et Droit International: Mélanges René-Jean Dupuy* (1991), p. 1, at 2, and discussion by Fassbender, "The United Nations Charter," 564.

[57] Dissenting opinion of Judge Alejandro Alvarez in the *Reservations to the Genocide Convention* case, International Court of Justice, [1951] ICJ Rep. 15, at 53 as cited by Fassbender, "The United Nations Charter," 595.

of the community, and even less to the views and consent of states. The sequence of this debate, involving so many questions relating to the basic principles and outlooks of international law, brings in the potential constitutional role of the International Court of Justice (ICJ) and of an independent Constitutional Court.

A constitutional role for the International Court of Justice

Some of the basic principles of international law are found today in the Charter of the United Nations and certain other major treaties. As interactions in the international society become more intense there will be an increasing need to identify and implement the essential principles of international law that govern such relations. New challenges in the field of international security and self-defense are just one example.

To identify those principles and their application to changing circumstances is to a large extent a judicial function, one that involves not only the interpretation of treaties but also a careful examination of customary law and the practice of states. As noted above, this exercise has a very specific constitutional dimension. Merrills has commented, "[s]ince international law is more controversial than domestic law, the international judge is more like a US Supreme Court justice, deciding a point of constitutional interpretation, than a domestic judge with a routine case."[58]

The question that needs to be asked is whether the International Court of Justice might perform a constitutional role in addition to its normal dispute settlement functions or in the context thereof.[59] The difficult issue of the reform of the Charter or of the ICJ itself will always be an obstacle in achieving this objective. However, one may start from the assumption that a number of changes are feasible without a thoroughgoing reform, i.e. without amending the Charter or the Statute, and that ultimately states may wish to undertake such steps.

[58] J.G. Merrills, *International Dispute Settlement* (1998), p. 294.

[59] For a discussion of these aspects see Francisco Orrego Vicuña and Christopher Pinto, *The Peaceful Settlement of Disputes: Prospects for the Twenty-first Century*, Final Report for the Centennial Commemoration of the First Peace Conference, May 1999, published in F. Kalhoven (ed.), *The Centennial of the First Peace Conference* (2000), p. 388 (hereinafter cited as Orrego Vicuña and Pinto, Report). On the role of the ICJ in keeping the coherence of the system of international law, see Jonathan I. Charney, "Third party dispute settlement and international law" 36 *Columbia Journal of Transnational Law* (1997) 65–89. See also Edward McWhinney, "The International Court as a Constitutional Court and the blurring of the arbitral/judicial processes" 6 *Leiden Journal of International Law* (1993) 279–295.

A more important obstacle arises from the fact that cases and disputes submitted to the International Court of Justice, like the Permanent Court of International Justice before it, do not always lend themselves to judicial decisions with a constitutional dimension.[60] Nonetheless both courts have been able to contribute to the development of the basic principles of international law by their judgments and advisory opinions. This may be more evident in matters involving technical aspects of international law, such as fisheries or maritime delimitation, than in questions that deal with major political issues, such as decolonization or the threat of use of nuclear weapons.

It must also be noted that the present system of consensual jurisdiction that is characteristic of the International Court of Justice is unlikely to change in the foreseeable future. As a consequence, states will continue to be reluctant to submit to it disputes involving critical political issues affecting domestic or international policies, which are also those where essential constitutional questions are raised.

Some important factors limit the capacity of the ICJ to perform a standing constitutional function in the world community. Prominent among them are: alternative dispute settlement arrangements made by states, the so-called proliferation of international tribunals, and the fact that questions relating to major areas of international law, such as those dealing with trade, finance and investments, are never brought by states before the court. To this extent, international law is becoming less structured, and even the meaning of some of its basic rules becomes less clear in the context of new international scenarios.

A new judicial policy by the ICJ would be required in order for it to assert a central role in the international community. This new role has been rightly described as one directed to "confirm and articulate the aggregate of principles of international law in respect of present conditions of international society, contributing more to the establishment and consolidation of the international legal system and even peaceful relations between States than a variety of cases dealing with secondary aspects which rather serve to inflate the statistics."[61] A number of proposals directed to strengthen the

---

[60] Shabtai Rosenne, "Lessons of the past and needs of the future" in Connie Peck and Roy S. Lee (eds.), *Increasing the Effectiveness of the International Court of Justice* (1997), pp. 466–492, at 468.

[61] Georges Abi-Saab, "De l'évolution de la Cour Internationale. Réflexions sur quelques tendances récentes" 2 *Revue Générale de Droit International Public* (1992) 273–297, at 295. Translation by this author.

judicial functions of the ICJ were made on the occasion of the Centennial Commemoration of the First Peace Conference,[62] the most important of which are outlined below:

(i) Acceptance of the compulsory jurisdiction of the ICJ should be explored in respect of a limited number of issues or matters,[63] in view of the fact that the consensual acceptance prevailing today as the general rule is unlikely to change. The present system of reservations to the optional clause could be streamlined. The current acceptance of compulsory jurisdiction in other dispute settlement arrangements dealing with specialized areas of the law, such as trade and investments, should be encouraged.

(ii) The advisory role of the International Court of Justice can also be developed as an effective mechanism to deal with questions involving the basic principles of international law. The Secretary General of the United Nations should be authorized to request advisory opinions on matters pertaining to his competence, ensuring that these requests do not interfere with the political functions of other bodies of the Organization.[64] Other organs of the United Nations and specialized agencies might be similarly empowered to the extent that they have a meaningful role within the system. Major regional organizations might also benefit from this authorization. States acting individually or jointly might also qualify for such an authorization within certain limits and in the context of established procedures for the settlement of disputes. Other proposals include institutional and procedural arrangements to facilitate the request of advisory opinions by the General Assembly, for example by lowering the required majorities.[65]

---

[62] Orrego Vicuña and Pinto, Report, and comments on these proposals by Pierre-Marie Dupuy, "The danger of fragmentation or unification of the international legal system and the International Court of Justice" 31 *New York University Journal of International Law and Politics* (1999) 791–807.

[63] See James Brown Scott, *The Reports of the Hague Conferences of 1899 and 1907* (1917), with reference to proposals on listings of matters for compulsory jurisdiction, and Louis B. Sohn, "Draft General Treaty on the Peaceful Settlement of International Disputes" 20 *The International Lawyer* (1986) 261, at 281–284. See also Shigeru Oda, "The compulsory jurisdiction of the International Court of Justice: a myth?" 49 *International and Comparative Law Quarterly* (2000) 251–277.

[64] United Nations Secretary-General, *An Agenda for Peace: Preventive Diplomacy, Peacemaking and Peace-keeping*, UN Doc. S/24111 (1992), para. 38, and comments by Stephen M. Schwebel, "Fifty years of the World Court: a critical appraisal" in *Proceedings of the American Society of International Law* (1996), pp. 339–347, at 347.

[65] Louis B. Sohn, Comments in Peck and Lee, *Increasing the Effectiveness*, p. 67.

(iii) Because on occasion non-governmental organizations and individuals have heavily politicized international law issues with which they are concerned, the suggestion that they also might request advisory opinions from the ICJ[66] does not seem viable, unless strict requirements of professionalism, accountability and transparency are first met.

(iv) The Charter's arrangements dealing with the maintenance of international peace and security could also be improved to provide for a new mutually reinforcing relationship between the International Court of Justice and the Security Council. Linking up in sequence the operation of Chapters VI and VII of the Charter could ensure a mutual referral of disputes between these two organs according to the prevalence of legal or political elements in the cases concerned.[67] In particular, an emphasis on prevention of disputes could enhance the participation of the principal organs of the United Nations in a concurrent effort to this end.

(v) The possibility of some form of *actio popularis* in respect of international community interests, that would allow the principal actors of the international system to take action before the ICJ when fundamental issues of international law are involved, also offers new grounds for the enhanced role of the court.[68] Any step in this direction, however, would require major safeguards so as to prevent the abuse of the procedure and its politicization.

(vi) Facilitating the access of international organizations to the contentious jurisdiction of the ICJ is another step that is in line with the enhanced participation of such entities in the international legal system.

(vii) A new role for the ICJ can also be envisaged in terms of the referral by other international tribunals,[69] or even by high domestic courts,[70] of questions of general international law arising before them. Again, a number of safeguards would have to be provided so as to prevent an

---

[66] M.C.W. Pinto, "The Court and other international tribunals" in Peck and Lee, *Increasing the Effectiveness*, pp. 281–309, at 292.

[67] Francisco Orrego Vicuña, "The settlement of disputes and conflict resolution in the context of a re-vitalized role for the United Nations Security Council" in R.-J. Dupuy (ed.), *The Development of the Role of the Security Council* (1993), p. 41, with reference to Brian Urquhart, *The United Nations: From Peace-Keeping to a Collective System?* (1991).

[68] Christine Chinkin, "Increasing the use and appeal of the Court" in Peck and Lee, *Increasing the Effectiveness*, pp. 50–55; Rosenne, "Lessons of the past," 488–489.

[69] Gilbert Guillaume, "The future of international judicial institutions" 44 *International and Comparative Law Quarterly* (1995) 848.

[70] Stephen M. Schwebel, "Preliminary rulings by the International Court of Justice at the instance of national courts" 28 *Virginia Journal of International Law* (1988) 495, and "Reply" by Rosenne in *ibid.* 29 (1989) 401.

abuse of the power to refer and to ensure the acceptance of the system by the tribunals concerned.

(viii) In conjunction with the above proposals, new institutional arrangements have been suggested to facilitate the work of the ICJ and of the other entities participating in the broader functions envisaged. Among these arrangements is a proposal to establish an Advocate General of the court,[71] whose function would be to present to the court the fundamental issues of international law and societal interests involved in the cases submitted. The establishment of a Special Committee of Legal Experts has also been suggested to help the development of these constitutional functions. The Committee could work with the United Nations Secretary General and other entities authorized to request advisory opinions, would report to the court on legal issues posed by such requests, and could even submit *amicus curiae* briefs. It could also cooperate with the United Nations Legal Counsel in the process of developing principles of international law.[72] The usefulness of these suggestions must be assessed in the context of the broader constitutional functions envisaged for the ICJ and its enhanced role.

Issue of judicial review and constitutional questions relating to the Security Council

As the Security Council has regained a central role in the management of the United Nations in terms of the maintenance of international peace and security, the constitutional debate has moved away from the General Assembly. As in most constitutional debates, political and legal issues are intertwined. Discussion concerning the powers of the Security Council involves legal considerations, including the doctrine of implied powers. But it also touches upon questions of legitimacy related to political views on the composition of the Council, the role of the permanent members, its enlargement and ultimately the reform of the United Nations and of the Charter as a whole. As explained above, to the extent that the discussion becomes politicized there is less hope of reaching a consensus on any possible approach.

The renewed activity of the Security Council is largely based on a liberal self-interpretation of its powers under Chapter VI of the Charter.[73] This cannot be discussed in any detail here. It must be noted, however, that there

[71] Chinkin, "Increasing the use," 52–56.　　[72] Orrego Vicuña and Pinto, Report.
[73] Dupuy, "Constitutional dimension," 25–28.

is a continuous enlargement of the concept of threats to the peace, particularly in terms of allowing for various forms of humanitarian intervention in domestic situations, to the point of its becoming a new feature of the action of the United Nations. At the same time there are new threats to the peace that remain largely ignored, despite their seriousness.

This uncertainty about its powers and functions has led to the identification of a "constitutional crisis" of the United Nations.[74] The most important crisis, however, has not originated within the United Nations and has not involved, as was assumed, the dissatisfaction of developing countries with the Security Council. It originated first in the collective decision of an important group of member states to use force in respect of an internal situation in a third country, namely in connection with the crisis in Kosovo, without any authorization or even prior consultation with the Security Council.[75] This crisis led to the questioning of the role of the United Nations by some of its most prominent members, including three of the permanent members of the Security Council.

The fact that this approach might have been to some extent legitimized *ex post facto* by the Council itself does not alter the impact of the precedent. Any major power or group of states could feel free in the future to pursue a course of action independent of the Security Council if it believes that this organ will not support its aims and if it has enough power to act independently. A different situation arose with the legitimate exercise of self-defense in Afghanistan in the context of the terrorist aggression against the USA. Here, the Council admitted the operation of the concept but in a sense failed to take prompt action to reaffirm its institutional role. As a result, the crisis of the United Nations has deepened. The situation of crisis only became more acute in connection with the events that followed in Iraq.

Constitutional discussion involving the Security Council has inevitably involved the issue of judicial review of its decisions by the International Court of Justice,[76] based on an analogy to the constitutional arrangements

---

[74] *Ibid.*, 25 with particular reference to Michael Reisman, "The constitutional crisis in the United Nations" 87 *American Journal of International Law* (1993) 83, and M. Bedjaoui, *Nouvel Ordre Mondial et contrôle de la légalité des actes du Conseil de Sécurité* (1994).

[75] For a discussion of the limits of the action undertaken by regional organizations and arrangements under the Charter, see Jorge Cardona Llorens, "La coopération entre les Nations Unies et les accords et organismes régionaux pour le réglément pacifique des affaires relatives au maintien de la paix et de la sécurité internationales" in *Boutros Boutros-Ghali Amicorum Discipulorumque Liber* (1998), pp. 251–289.

[76] Alvarez, "Judging the Security Council"; M. Bedjaoui, "Du contrôle de la légalité des actes du Conseil de Sécurité" in *Recueil d'études en l'honneur du professeur François Rigaux* (1993), pp. 69–110; D. Bowett, "The impact of Security Council decisions on dispute

of some domestic legal systems. The federal experience in respect of judicial review as initially expressed in *Marbury* v. *Madison*[77] has led some authors to suggest the introduction of checks and balances in the work of the organs of the United Nations. This is another issue where there is a clash between the realists, who support the uncontrolled powers of the Security Council, and the legalists who see the opportunity for an intervention by the International Court of Justice to safeguard the legitimacy of the system.[78]

The prospect is certainly not within close reach, given the exclusive powers conferred upon the Security Council by Chapter VI of the Charter, the difficult political balances within the United Nations system and the lack of express authority for the ICJ to perform any related functions.[79] The analogy of an "executive," "legislative" and "judicial" branch within the United Nations has also been questioned, just as has the constitutional nature of the Charter and the very existence of an international community.[80]

It is evident that the Charter provides for no arrangement granting any organ control over the Security Council. The Charter provides for no clear separation of powers or a system of checks and balances. Any development as outlined above would not only mean the introduction of a fundamental legal innovation in the Charter's system but also a major political rearrangement. The question is raised again whether it could be done without the express consent of the members of the Organization.

Models of judicial review based on federal experience or on judicial review in the European Communities are therefore not appropriate for consideration in respect of the International Court of Justice. In fact, it has been rightly commented that such federal judicial precedent is misleading in the case of the ICJ as it concerns a totally different institutional setting.[81] However, in spite of numerous doubts, the fact is that the

---

settlement procedures", 89 *European Journal of International Law* (1994) 5; L. Caflisch, "Is the International Court of Justice entitled to review Security Council resolutions adopted under Chapter VII of the United Nations Charter?" in N. Al-Nauimi and R. Meese (eds.), *International Legal Issues Arising Under the United Nations Decade of International Law* (1995), p. 633; Dapo Akande, "The International Court of Justice and the Security Council: is there room for judicial control of decisions of the political organs of the United Nations?" 46 *International and Comparative Law Quarterly* (1997) 309–343; K. Skubiszewski, "The ICJ and the Security Council" in *Fifty Years of the International Court of Justice: Essays in Honour of Sir Robert Jennings* (1996), p. 616.

[77] *Marbury* v. *Madison*, 5 U.S. (1 Cranch) 137, 1803.
[78] Alvarez, "Judging the Security Council," 2–3, with reference to the contemporary debate on the subject.
[79] Orrego Vicuña and Pinto, Report.
[80] See generally Arangio-Ruiz, "The 'federal analogy.'"
[81] Alvarez, "Judging the Security Council," 4–6.

examination of the legality of Security Council decisions has become an issue. The International Court of Justice has dealt with it in both *Bosnia*[82] and *Lockerbie*,[83] and the International Criminal Tribunal for the Former Yugoslavia (ICTY) has done so in the *Tadic* case.[84] The very discussion of the action by the Security Council on these occasions involves an exercise in judicial review independent of the absence of a negative conclusion on its consistency with the Charter and its validity.[85]

The function of judicial review must be considered separately from the institutionalization of the mechanism of judicial review. The International Court of Justice will always be in a position to examine the legality of decisions of the Security Council or any other body that are brought before it in the context of legal arguments made by the parties, or, in an advisory opinion, by those states and international organizations appearing before it. Other courts may be specifically prohibited to do so, as in the case with the Sea-bed Disputes Chamber of the International Tribunal for the Law of the Sea. As noted by Judge Jennings, the function of judicial review may be accomplished "without it amounting to a step towards the establishment of a 'system of judicial review.'"[86] To institutionalize a mechanism or a system of judicial review is a different matter, as it involves the recognition of the supremacy of an organ over another and granting it the authority to declare decisions null and void.

The question, as put by Jennings, is how to approach cases where constitutional principles of international organization and law are involved. His suggested approach is "to eschew large *a priori* assumptions of principle, and proceed by a case by case method of gradually building up a body of legal rules and principles based firmly upon the practical experience of decisions suited to particular cases as they arise."[87] This is indeed an accepted judicial function that does not involve institutional superiority, any explicit declaration of nullity of decisions of any other body, or indeed any institutional interference whatever. Most importantly, it is likely to be taken into account

---

[82] *Application of the Convention on the Prevention and Punishment of the Crime of Genocide (Bosnia-Herzegovina v. Yugoslavia (Serbia and Montenegro))*, Provisional Measures, [1993] ICJ Rep. 3 (Order of 8 April), and [1993] ICJ Rep. 325 (Order of 13 September).

[83] *Questions of Interpretation and Application of the 1971 Montreal Convention arising from the Aerial Incident at Lockerbie (Libya v. UK, Libya v. US)*, Provisional Measures, [1992] ICJ Rep. 3, 114 (Order of 14 April).

[84] *The Prosecutor v. Dusko Tadic* (Case No. IT-94-1-AR72), 2 October 1995, para. 43.

[85] Orrego Vicuña and Pinto, Report.

[86] Robert Y. Jennings, "The role of the International Court of Justice" 68 *British Year Book of International Law* (1997) 1–63, at 52.

[87] *Ibid.*, 52.

by other bodies that will consider or decide similar questions subsequently. It is simply a question of the correct application of the law in a specific case based upon the essential underlying principles that the court has identified, step by step.

Such a function may be exercised in the course of contentious proceedings or, more often, in the context of advisory opinions to the extent that issues arise relating to the principles of international law or organization. Requests for advisory opinions need not result from the existence of a dispute but may simply reflect the need for independent interpretation of rules or principles. The expansion of the advisory jurisdiction would allow for a broader access to the ICJ so that it could exercise this type of functional judicial review. It has been noted that this is not only a judicial function: a number of United Nations bodies, such as the Human Rights Commission and the United Nations Compensation Commission, regularly apply, and to this extent interpret, Security Council decisions.[88]

This type of function may be developed by the International Court of Justice which is likely to exercise it more often as the Security Council generates more law and takes more actions involving legal considerations.[89] It may even be a very viable mode to articulate community goals and objectives that are otherwise not expressly stated under international law.[90] These aspects are not unknown to the work of the ICJ. The development, identification and application of the basic principles of international law are not limited to questions of unconstitutionality of a decision and hence do not require a rearrangement of roles under the Charter, still less any amendment.

A constitutional court for the world community

The International Court of Justice has dealt with the principles of international law and will continue to do so. To that extent it may increasingly become a constitutional court, particularly if the changes suggested above are introduced. However, there are two limits to this function of the court. First, the ICJ itself may not wish to develop this role. It may feel that this would go beyond its mandate under the Charter or affect its relationship with the Security Council, or the role of the five permanent members, who are represented in the court. Second, as noted above, the most important constitutional challenges for the United Nations, and for the development of

[88] Alvarez, "Judging the Security Council," 8–11.   [89] *Ibid.*, 20.
[90] *Ibid.*, 30–34. See also generally M. Weller, "The reality of the emerging Universal Constitutional Order" X *Cambridge Review of International Affairs* (1997), 41.

principles of international law, do not come from within the Organization, but from the outside. In this respect, the ICJ might not be in a position to develop a constitutional role, or it may never get an opportunity to do so.

Either way, the possibility exists that one day states may consider the establishment of a constitutional court that would function independently of the United Nations, but have necessary links with the Organization. Discussions on this proposal were held on the occasion of the Centennial Commemoration of the First Peace Conference and concluded with a temporizing recommendation that it should be subject to further study. It was also noted that the International Court of Justice already fulfils a constitutional role within the United Nations system, protecting it from disintegration; on the other hand, it was pointed out that in many domestic legal systems a Constitutional Court and a Supreme Court exist side by side.[91]

Indeed, the view was expressed that a prerequisite for a Constitutional Court is the existence of a constitution. However, the considerations set out above in respect of a constitutional role or function dealing with the basic principles of international law show that there is no need to have a formal constitution, because the principles themselves assume this role, step by step. Domestic experiences also show that there is not always a need for a constitution in order to develop basic or constitutional principles organizing the essential aspects of social order. The example of the United Kingdom shows that a written constitution is not necessary.

Because the constitutional elements of international law deal with substantive principles of law and not necessarily with institutional questions, there is no need for this function to be associated with an institutional structure, such as that of the United Nations. Nor does it have to be concerned with the allocation of competences between different entities, as is the case with most domestic constitutional arrangements.[92]

There is also no need for it to be associated with the idea of constitutional supremacy that is typical of domestic constitutional systems. Constitutional principles of international law do not require the establishment of a "world state"[93] because they are unrelated to the exercise of sovereignty. In this respect, it has been rightly noted that there is no compelling reason to reserve the term "constitution" for the constitution of a state.[94]

---

[91] *United Nations Decade of International Law: Outcome of the Celebrations of the Centennial of the First International Peace Conference: Report of the Conclusions*, The Hague 17–18 May 1999, St. Petersburg, 22–25 June 1999, para. 113.

[92] See note 32, and associated text.   [93] Fassbender, "The United Nations Charter," 558.

[94] *Ibid.*, 556.

Moreover, because international law is fundamentally a horizontal system of law, the constitutional dimension is not directed at introducing any more verticality than that accepted by the community of states. In this connection, it may well be that a Constitutional Court could reaffirm the basic principles of equality of states under international law and the requirements of state consent for the elaboration or development of international legal rules. Much of the so-called verticality of the law has not been judicially tested and in many cases is the outcome of intellectual perceptions, not the result of the will of states or other subjects of international law.

This is not the occasion to discuss the jurisdiction of such a court or its organization. It is only necessary to keep in mind that it should be able to decide on the meaning and extent of fundamental principles and questions of interpretation, submitted by states and other entities. To this end one could envisage both a contentious and an advisory jurisdiction and a rather broad access to the court. Controversial decisions of domestic courts on principles of international law might also be brought before the court for review.

As concerns the organization of the court, it should avoid the problems that have confronted the International Court of Justice in terms of its composition and election, representation and working methods. To this end, the court should be broadly representative of the international community and have a close connection with major regional organizations.

A Constitutional Court for the world community, or the International Court of Justice in this renewed role, would be the best guarantee that international law will continue to evolve in an orderly and coherent manner. International society would thereby avoid dispersion and fragmentation and, above all, would ensure that it will not take a course contrary to the will of the community as has happened only too often in the past.

3

Individuals and settlement of international claims: change and adaptation of governing rules

An inherent right to bring claims and seek remedies under international law

Just as the developments in international society relating to decentralization suggest the need for a centralized court to ensure the constitutional unity of such society, so too the process of globalization requires that participants in the system have adequate access to international dispute settlement. The significant participation of individuals and corporations in the global society creates a need for them to have access to dispute settlement, which thus far has been only a limited feature of the inter-state system.

The view that only states are subjects of international law is no longer sustainable either in theory or practice.[1] The opposite view, that individuals are the sole subjects of international law,[2] while perhaps more attractive as a matter of legal theory, has not found support in an international society where states and international organizations participate as entities endowed with international personality. It is no longer disputed that individuals have international personality and may be direct beneficiaries of rights, as well as have duties, under international law.[3] But there is still a major unsettled question in respect of their capacity to exercise these rights and to be held responsible for their duties in the international legal system.

[1] For a critical analysis of the views of Anzilotti, Triepel, Strupp and other authors affirming the exclusive international personality of the state, see Marek St. Korowicz, "The problem of the international personality of individuals" 50 *American Journal of International Law* (1956) 533–562, at 541–542.
[2] For a critical analysis of the views of Duguit, Politis, Scelle and Kelsen on the international personality of individuals, see *ibid.*, 539–540.
[3] For a discussion of the opinion by Brierly in respect of the role of the individual, see *ibid.*, 537.

As has been pointed out, "[l]egal personality is an acknowledgement that an entity is capable of exercising certain rights and being subject to certain duties on its own account under a particular system of law."[4] To the extent that individuals are prevented from claiming and seeking remedies or from being held responsible directly under international law, that is, from standing on their own account, their international personality will be somewhat nominal and lacking in effectiveness. Many authors and international tribunals have made the distinction "between the possession of rights and duties and the procedural capacity to sue or be sued on them."[5] The purpose of this distinction is mainly to justify considering the individual as a subject while admitting that individuals may only be able to assert claims with their national government as an intermediary. The end result is a "diminished" international personality. Indeed, as Judge Higgins has commented, "Lord Denning thought in the *Gouriet* case that a right which depended for its enforcement upon the consent of another party was close to being no legal right at all."[6]

In the light of this changing role of states, international organizations, individuals and other entities in the international legal system, the traditional distinction between subjects and objects of international law has also become less meaningful and practical. What really matters is whether an entity or individual genuinely participates in the system of international law,[7] acting pursuant to rules binding across national borders. When this is the case, the access of such participants to international dispute settlement in order to bring a claim and enforce a right should be recognized without difficulty. The nature of international law itself poses no obstacle to such access,[8] but there is a constant need to adapt the rules of the system to these new realities. There is also a clear need to establish the limits and requirements of such a broadened system so as to prevent abuses that could result in the distortion of the very purpose of the changes introduced.

This chapter will examine the first major line of change and adaptation that is taking place: that concerning the traditional rule of the nationality of claims. This rule used to be, and to some extent still is, a tool enabling

---

[4] P.K. Menon, "The subjects of modern international law" 3 *Hague Yearbook of International Law* (1990) 30–86, at 31.

[5] C. Nørgaard, *The Position of the Individual in International Law* (1962), with reference to a decision of the Permanent Court of International Justice, Series A/B No. 61, p. 231, as cited by Rosalyn Higgins, "Conceptual thinking about the individual in international law" in Falk, Kratochwil and Mendlovitz (eds.), *International Law: A Contemporary Perspective* (1985), pp. 476–494, at 479. See also Francesco Durante, *Ricorsi individuali ad organi internazionali: contributo alla teoria della personalità internazionale dell'individuo* (1958).

[6] Higgins, "Conceptual thinking," 479.   [7] *Ibid.*, 480.   [8] *Ibid.*, 477–479.

governments and states to control the process of international claims involving individuals, corporations and other private entities. Other major lines of change will be examined separately. They include the precedents established in the twentieth century relating to direct access of individuals to international dispute settlement, as well as certain specialized mechanisms open to participation by individuals and corporations.

All of the above indicates a new trend in dispute settlement under international law, one where access of individuals and corporations to international claims and remedies is gradually being recognized as a right inherent in their possession of international personality.

Asserting the rights of individuals: changing approaches to the law relating to nationality of claims

As Bennouna rightly pointed out in the International Law Commission, an important question in the context of diplomatic protection and the requirements of nationality is that of whose rights are asserted when an international claim is brought.[9] Traditional rules governing this are today being challenged because of the need to provide different solutions in light of new realities.[10]

The classic rule in the matter was laid down in the *Mavrommatis Palestine Concessions* case, where the Permanent Court of International Justice ruled that "[b]y taking up the case of one of its subjects and by resorting to diplomatic action or international judicial proceedings on his behalf, a State is in reality asserting its own rights – its right to ensure, in the person of its subjects, respect for the rules of international law."[11] As explained by Bennouna, this conceptual approach led to a "transformation" of the claim, which passed from the individual to the espousing state of nationality; as a result the role of the state became paramount and eclipsed that of the

---

[9] International Law Commission, *Preliminary Report on Diplomatic Protection*, by Mohammed Bennouna, Special Rapporteur, A/CN 4/484, 4 February 1998, p. 5. See also Georges Scelle, "Droit de la paix" 46 IV *Recueil des Cours de l'Academie de Droit International* (1933) 660–661, as cited by Bennouna, *ibid.*, 8, note 18. See also International Law Commission, *First Report on Diplomatic Protection*, by John R. Dugard, Special Rapporteur, A/CN 4/506, 7 March 2000, pp. 12–13, 24–25.

[10] Francisco Orrego Vicuña, *The Changing Law of Nationality of Claims*, Report for the International Law Association Committee on Diplomatic Protection of Persons and Property, Sixty-Ninth Conference (London, 2000), pp. 631–647, on which this chapter is based in part (hereinafter cited as Orrego Vicuña, ILA Report).

[11] *Mavrommatis Palestine Concessions, Permanent Court of International Justice*, Series A No. 2, 30 August 1924.

individual which had been at its origin.[12] Discretionary espousal of claims, disposition of the compensation by the state, introduction of a type of damage different from that suffered by the individual, and the influence of political power, were some of the inevitable consequences of this approach.[13]

A number of legal contradictions have accompanied this approach since the beginning. First, in cases where direct injury to a state could be established, international law provided for different rules of protection, such as rules relating to self-protection.[14] The requirement of continuity of nationality of the affected individual also involved a contradiction since "[i]t is also illogical to consider the State as the sole holder of the international claim, yet at the same time to prevent the State from pursuing this claim because the 'nationality' of the underlying individual claim has changed."[15] Nor did diplomatic protection follow the evolution that the law of state responsibility was experiencing in important respects.[16]

However, it was the very structure of international law that led to fundamental changes in the role of diplomatic protection. As states lost their exclusivity as actors in the international legal order, and both international organizations and individuals acquired specific, albeit still limited, roles of their own, new alternatives emerged for the assertion of international claims. Precedents established in the twentieth century, allowing for direct access of individuals to international mechanisms, dispensed with diplomatic protection altogether.

But even where a state intervenes in the exercise of diplomatic protection, it is often the right of the individual, not that of the state of nationality, which is asserted. The state may still act as a conduit, an agent or on behalf of the individual, but no longer in substitution of the individual's rights. This is not to say that the state may not consider that a wrong done to one of its nationals affects its own interests. In the course of the transition from legal fiction to a different reality, the interesting idea has been advanced that a claim may actually have a "dual nature" and represent the interests of both the individual and the state.[17]

---

[12] International Law Commission, *Preliminary Report on Diplomatic Protection*, p. 5.

[13] *Ibid.*, pp. 6–7.

[14] Wilhelm Karl Geck, "Diplomatic Protection" in *Encyclopedia of Public International Law* (1992), p. 1046.

[15] *Ibid.*, p. 1056.

[16] Institut de Droit International, Resolution on Responsibility and Liability under International Law for Environmental Damage, 4 September 1997, 67–11 *Annuaire de l'Institut de Droit International*, Session de Strasbourg (1998) 487.

[17] Comments by Professor J. Kokott to Orrego Vicuña, ILA Report.

However, the argument diminishing the importance of diplomatic protection must not be pushed too far. In fact, the option of abolishing diplomatic protection as a mechanism under international law, while justified in the context of specific treaty regimes, does not seem reasonable at present. This step would result in many individuals unprotected or left to act on their own, and would be self-defeating. In spite of the inconveniences noted, the present system has the advantage of an orderly administration of claims by the state of nationality, the availability of diplomatic channels for negotiations and settlement, and the intervention of such state in the implementation of legal rules.[18]

A residual role for diplomatic protection seems more appropriate, allowing that mechanism to become engaged when there are no international procedures directly available to the affected individual.[19] On the other hand, if direct access is available, diplomatic protection should be excluded altogether, except perhaps in order to ensure the enforcement of an award or secure compliance with a decision favoring that individual. In particular, there would be no question of diplomatic protection after the individual resorts to international procedures or in lieu thereof.

Another aspect of the problem of the individual's rights relates to a question of due process in the context of diplomatic protection. To the extent that the decision to espouse a claim is fully discretionary, a government may simply refuse to accept the individual's request and no remedies will be available. It would be helpful, in order to avoid undue interference with the rights of the individual, if such decisions were subject to a process of legal scrutiny or judicial review.[20]

A more flexible link of nationality

The requirement of a genuine and effective link of nationality for the purpose of sponsoring international claims as laid down in the *Nottebohm* case[21] is a well established rule of international law, one that has been strengthened

---

[18] Comments by Lady Fox to Orrego Vicuña, ILA Report.

[19] For a discussion of these options, see *ibid.*

[20] An interesting historical solution to this problem is found in the Chilean legislation of the nineteenth century, where the request for diplomatic protection would be sent by the Ministry of Foreign Affairs to the Advocate General (Fiscal) of the Supreme Court for a legal opinion that was binding on the government. See Francisco Orrego Vicuña, "Chile" in Elihu Lauterpacht and John G. Collier, *Individual Rights and the State in Foreign Affairs* (1977), pp. 123–186, at 139–140.

[21] [1955] ICJ Rep. 4, at 23.

in a number of additional areas.[22] However, the needs of the evolving legal order are leading to some changes in the operation of this rule.

In a number of cases, departure from a treaty rule has allowed states to sponsor claims of persons who did not have the nationality of the sponsoring state.[23] It has also been noted that since the claiming state had discretion as to the distribution of compensation, it could make payments to persons who did not meet the requirement of nationality.[24] A declaration of intention to acquire the nationality of the claiming state has also been considered sufficient to espouse the claim. Claims on behalf of non-nationals are not unknown in the practice of international law.[25] Citizens of the European Union are entitled to diplomatic and consular assistance by the authorities of any Member State in the territory of a third country in which the state of the individual is not represented. However, this type of protection is related more to consular or diplomatic assistance *in situ* than to the possibility of presenting an international claim.[26]

Two other situations need to be considered in this context. The first concerns claims made on behalf of nationals of the defendant state. An early precedent set in this respect by the *I'm Alone* case[27] was developed in an agreement between Chile and the USA settling the dispute concerning the responsibility for the deaths of *Letelier and Moffitt*,[28] where "[t]he Chilean nationality or dual nationality of some of the persons protected by the United States Government was not raised as a bar to the disposition of the corresponding claims . . . which in actual fact means that the

---

[22] See, e.g., the United Nations Convention on the Law of the Sea, Art. 91; FAO, Agreement to Promote Compliance with International Conservation and Management Measures by Fishing Vessels on the High Seas, 24 November 1993, (1994) 33 *International Legal Materials* 968, Art. III.3.

[23] Robert Jennings and Arthur Watts (eds.), *Oppenheim's International Law* (1992), vol. 1, p. 513.

[24] *Ibid.*, p. 513.

[25] *Reparation for Injuries Suffered in the Service of the United Nations* [1949] ICJ Rep. 174, where the ICJ stated that there are "important exceptions to the rule, for there are cases in which protection may be exercised by a State on behalf of persons not having its nationality," at 181. For contemporary practice on diplomatic protection of foreign nationals see Rudolf Dolzer, "Diplomatic Protection of Foreign Nationals" in *Encyclopedia of Public International Law* (1992), pp. 1067–1070. See further International Law Commission, *First Report on Diplomatic Protection*, Art. 5 and comments thereto, pp. 34–41.

[26] Article 8c of the European Community Treaty, as cited in comments by Kokott to Orrego Vicuña, ILA Report.

[27] RIAA, III, 1935, at 1609, and comments in Oppenheim's *International Law* (1992), p. 513, note 8.

[28] Agreement between Chile and the USA of 11 June 1990, (1991) 30 *International Legal Materials* 412.

humanitarian concerns have prevailed over the traditional requirements [of diplomatic protection]."[29] The latter case also showed that the USA did not substitute its interest for that of the families protected, acting only on their behalf.[30] Consequently, it was the right of the individuals and not that of the claiming state that was enforced, with the state acting in effect as a surrogate or even in a fiduciary capacity so far as concerns the handling of compensation.[31]

A second situation concerns cases where some state other than the state of nationality espouses or otherwise supports a claim. A foreign national is often allowed to bring claims before the courts of the defendant state; in some cases it may even bring those claims before courts of a third state,[32] a policy that has been encouraged on non-discriminatory terms under the OECD.[33] In such cases the state of nationality would probably not be allowed to sue in domestic courts on behalf of the individual. An example is the European Union where direct access has been recognized. A separate problem is that of sovereign immunity, but, as will be shown below, there have been many intervening changes in this respect.[34] The possibility of claiming on behalf of non-nationals in the United Nations Compensation Commission will also be examined. Second, special forms of protection have also been recognized in the case of stateless persons.[35] Special rules have

---

[29] Decision of the Chile-United States Commission with regard to the dispute concerning responsibility for the deaths of Letelier and Moffitt, 11 January 1992, Separate Concurrent Opinion of Commissioner Francisco Orrego Vicuña, (1992) 31 *International Legal Materials* 17–18.

[30] *Ibid.*, Separate Opinion, at 18.   [31] *Ibid.*, at 18.

[32] American Law Institute, Restatement of the Law Third, *The Foreign Relations Law of the United States* (1987), vol. 1, p. 223 (hereinafter cited as Foreign Relations Law of the United States).

[33] OECD, Recommendation of the Council for the Implementation of a Regime of Equal Right of Access and Non-discrimination in relation to Transfrontier Pollution, 17 May 1977, (1977) 16 *International Legal Materials* 977.

[34] Cf. *Al-Adsani* v. *United Kingdom*, Application 35763/97, Decision as to Admissibility of 1 March 2000, Judgment of 21 November 2001; *Fogarty* v. *United Kingdom*, Application 37112/97, Decision as to Admissibility of 1 March 2000, Judgment of 21 November 2001; *McElhinney* v. *Ireland*, Application 31253/96, Decision as to Admissibility of 9 February 2000, Judgment of 21 November 2001. In each of these three cases, the applicants brought complaints before the European Court of Human Rights after national courts/tribunals had rejected their claims against alleged offending states on the basis of the doctrine of sovereign immunity. In all three cases, the European Court of Human Rights rejected the applicants' contentions that such rejection effectively constituted a denial of access to court contrary to Art. 6(1) of the European Convention for the Protection of Human Rights and Fundamental Freedoms.

[35] Convention relating to the Status of Stateless Persons, and comments in Foreign Relations Law of the United States, vol. 1, p. 218.

also been provided under the Convention on the Nationality of Women,[36] including situations of change of nationality because of marriage and in respect of military service in cases of double nationality,[37] as well as other special situations.[38]

These cases demonstrate that the link of nationality has to some extent lost its rigor in the context of international claims. Moreover, the link of nationality will lose its relevance to the extent that the intervention of the state is reduced or eliminated as a requirement for submission of international claims. This is not to say that traditional requirements have been overturned, but it certainly indicates greater flexibility and adaptation to changing needs.

Adapting the rule of continuous nationality

A second well-established rule in respect of diplomatic protection is that of continuous nationality. As proposed by Garcia Amador, the individual may be protected on condition that he or she possesses the nationality of the espousing state "at the time of sustaining the injury and conserves that nationality until the claim is adjudicated."[39] The requirement of continuous nationality until the presentation of the claim[40] seems hitherto to have been favored by state practice.[41] As pointed out above, if in the context of the traditional approach to diplomatic protection, the rights of the individual were no longer upheld after injury is suffered, and only those of the state, there would be an apparent contradiction in requiring that the individual's nationality should continue.

Thus it is necessary to ask whether the rule is justified in the context of the new approach to diplomatic protection, where it is increasingly the

---

[36] Convention on the Nationality of Women, TS No. 875 (1934), and comments in Foreign Relations Law of the United States, vol. 1, p. 118.

[37] Protocol relating to Military Obligations in Certain Cases of Double Nationality, 1930, TS No. 913.

[38] Convention establishing the Status of Naturalized Persons who Again Take up Residence in the Country of their Origin, TS No. 575 (1908) and comments in Foreign Relations Law of the United States, vol. 1, p. 118.

[39] See the revised draft prepared by F.V. García Amador on State Responsibility for the International Law Commission, 1961, in F.V. García Amador, *The Changing Law of International Claims* (1984), vol. II, p. 795, Art. 23; see also the Draft Convention on International Responsibility prepared by Professors Louis B. Sohn and Richard R. Baxter for the Harvard Law School, 1961, in García Amador, *ibid.*, p. 858, Art. 23.7.

[40] *Oppenheim's International Law*, p. 512. See also the discussion of the rule by G. Schwarzenberger, *International Law as Applied by International Courts and Tribunals* (1957), p. 597, and comments in García Amador, *The Changing Law*, p. 504.

[41] *Encyclopedia of International Law*, p. 1055.

right of the individual, and not that of the state acting on the individual's behalf, that is upheld and enforced. In the view of some scholars there are strong reasons to favor the continuance of nationality, particularly because of its role in the allocation of claims among various espousing states and in helping to avoid conflicts of interest.[42] This would help to eliminate the uncertainties that otherwise could affect the practice of international claims.[43]

The opposite conclusion, however, may be equally justified. In fact, if the right of the individual is affected, the relevant critical date is that of the wrong, and a subsequent change of nationality should not have any effect in this respect. The wrong "follows" the individual in question. As Lowe points out, if the date of the injury is the critical date for questions of nationality there is a good reason for it to be determinative in respect of questions of jurisdiction of the tribunal.[44]

Sohn and Baxter hinted at these different approaches in the Draft Convention of 1961 when they said that "[a] State shall not be precluded from presenting a claim on behalf of a person by reason of the fact that that person became a national of that State subsequent to that injury."[45] A draft prepared by the American Institute of International Law in 1925 recognized the right of a state to accord diplomatic protection "to its native or naturalized citizens," not excluding the possibility that the latter might have been injured before their naturalization.[46]

An example of the practical application of this solution is the *Helms-Burton Act* of 1996, which not only allows claims by US nationals deprived of property in Cuba but also by such nationals who at the time of the expropriation were Cuban citizens.[47] The Act not only includes an exception to the rule of continuance of nationality but also makes available claims procedures to former nationals of the wrongdoing state, although such claims are directed against governments, companies or individuals engaged in business relating to the confiscated properties.

The strict retention of the rule of continuance of nationality no longer finds justification in the light of the changing role of nationality as a requirement of diplomatic protection. There is here a need to revise or at any rate to adjust the operation of the rule to the new reality.

[42] Comments by Lady Fox to Orrego Vicuña, ILA Report.
[43] Comments by Professor Bederman to Orrego Vicuña, ILA Report.
[44] Comments by Professor Lowe to Orrego Vicuña, ILA Report.
[45] Sohn and Baxter, Draft Convention, in García Amador, *The Changing Law*, p. 6, Art. 23.
[46] Projects on State Responsibility of the American Institute of International Law, 1925, Art. II, in García Amador, *The Changing Law*, p. 826.
[47] United States House of Representatives, Report No. 104–202, p. 31.

Transferability of claims in the global market

The continuance of nationality has been generally required also in respect of the transferability of claims, particularly in matters of succession on death, assignment, insurance subrogation, etc.[48] Again the question whether this rule is always justified in the light of a new approach to diplomatic protection and the enforcement of claims arises. If the right of the individual prevails, it would seem enough for the right to a claim to be established at a critical date, while subsequent changes of nationality should not be an obstacle to future claims.

To some degree this situation was recognized in claims to property beneficially owned by one person, where the nominal title to such property was vested in another person of a different nationality. Usually, it was the nationality of the former that prevailed for the purposes of the claim.[49] The question is even more relevant with respect to insurance claims, because the rights of the insured may pass to the insurer by way of subrogation.[50] The continuance of nationality is probably no longer justified in the light of a global insurance market, in which the insured and the insurer will often have different nationalities. Investment insurance, such as that available under OPIC or MIGA, is also based on subrogation of rights.[51]

Although the traditional rule on this point is still regarded as universally accepted, there are solid grounds for departure from it in some matters, or at least for introducing some flexibility. The globalization of financial and service markets will probably require a departure from the rule. In fact, the application of the traditional rule in the context of globally structured financial markets – where shares, bonds and other instruments constantly and speedily change hands, and consequently nationality – can only be regarded as an anachronism. This could result in given instances in depriving legitimate owners and investors of protection on the part of states of nationality.

In one ICSID case the question of international transfer of promissory notes was considered. The protection of a foreign investor as the transferee of those notes was upheld by the tribunal in the light of the nature of global markets.[52] It might also be appropriate to ensure that the transfer of claims be made *bona fide* so as to prevent the transfer of a claim to a national of a

---

[48] *Oppenheim's International Law*, p. 514.   [49] *Ibid.*, p. 514.   [50] *Ibid.*, p. 514.
[51] Foreign Relations Law of the United States, vol. 1, p. 227.
[52] *Fedax N.V. v. Republic of Venezuela*, 11 July 1997, ICSID, (1998) 37 *International Legal Materials* 1378.

stronger state in order to strengthen diplomatic protection, a concern that has been often expressed.[53]

Double nationality revisited

The traditional rules, laid down in the 1930 Hague Convention on Certain Questions Relating to the Conflict of Nationality Laws,[54] require that a state should not be allowed to present a claim on behalf of a national when such person is also a national of the respondent state. Even if this rule is somehow qualified by criteria relating to the closer connection of the individual with the respondent state or with a third state of nationality, it does not appear today to be quite as consolidated as was once thought.[55]

In fact, as noted above, in a number of cases diplomatic protection has been exercised in respect of nationals of the defendant state who also had the nationality of the claiming state. If the connection of the dual national with the claiming state is stronger, departure from the rule has been readily recognized by international decisions.[56] The possibility that a state might accept, by treaty, the obligation to provide to all persons within its jurisdiction, regardless of nationality, a standard of protection required by that treaty has also been envisaged. In this situation nationality will cease to be relevant, as often happens in treaties of economic integration or trade liberalization.[57]

There is even more reason to allow such flexibility when the dual nationality involves a third state, a situation in which the effectiveness of the link of nationality will have a greater weight. The practice of the Iran-United States Claims Tribunal offers interesting insights into the new issues and problems relating to the rules on dual nationality.[58] The criteria according

---

[53] *Encyclopedia of International Law*, p. 1056.

[54] For a discussion of these provisions, see *Encyclopedia of International Law*, p. 1050.

[55] See the discussion in *Oppenheim's International Law*, pp. 516–517. In the Advisory Opinion on the Reparation for Injuries Suffered in the Service of the United Nations, the ICJ considered that the practice of a state not to protect a national against another state which also regards him as a national is "the ordinary practice," [1949] ICJ Rep. 174, at 186.

[56] See in particular the Mergé Claim (1955) 22 International Law Reports 443, and discussion of this and other cases in *Oppenheim's International Law*, p. 516; see also Foreign Relations Law of the United States, vol. 1, p. 218.

[57] Comments by Lady Fox to Orrego Vicuña, ILA Report.

[58] See below. See also the comments by Lowe to Orrego Vicuña, ILA Report. See also *Oppenheim's International Law*, p. 516.

to which such effectiveness should be evaluated will depend on the circumstances of each case, where residence, family ties, property, taxation and many other elements will determine the "stronger social bond of attachment."[59] Joint action by two states of nationality in respect of a third state has also been suggested as an alternative when both are willing to extend their diplomatic protection to the affected individual.[60]

Thus the traditional rules of the 1930 Convention are being applied with a greater degree of flexibility, which will become particularly marked in connection with the approach to diplomatic protection relying on the rights of the individual as the prevailing element.

Nationality of corporations: by-passing *Barcelona Traction*

Except for a corporation incorporated under the laws of the claiming state whose majority of shareholders are nationals of that state, in which case diplomatic protection will not be questioned,[61] in every other situation there may be difficulties with the traditional requirements of nationality. A number of other criteria have been used to determine the right to diplomatic protection, in particular, domicile, *siège social* or principal place of management and control.[62] These additional criteria have been rightly described not as conferring nationality, but as creating an equivalent connection sufficient for the exercise of diplomatic protection.[63]

One of the most problematic aspects of the matter was submitted to the International Court of Justice in the *Barcelona Traction* case[64] and concerned the right of a state to protect shareholders of its nationality in a foreign corporation affected by measures of a third state. While the *dictum* of the court was in the negative and the right to diplomatic protection was recognized only in respect of the state of incorporation, criticism of this decision and subsequent practice evidence that the question was not really settled at the

---

[59] See generally Institut de Droit International, Resolution on the National Character of an International Claim Presented by a State for Injury Suffered by an Individual, 10 September 1965, *Annuaire*, Vol. 51-II, 1965, at 260. See also International Law Commission, *First Report on Diplomatic Protection*, Arts 6 and 7 and comments thereto, pp. 42–57.

[60] Comments by Kokott to Orrego Vicuña, ILA Report, with reference to C. Warbrick, "Protection of nationals abroad", Current Legal Problems, 37 *International and Comparative Law Quarterly* (1988) 1003, 1006. See also International Law Commission, *First Report on Diplomatic Protection*, Art. 7.2.

[61] *Oppenheim's International Law*, pp. 517–518.

[62] García Amador, *The Changing Law*, pp. 508–512.

[63] Foreign Relations Law of the United States, vol. 1, p. 213.

[64] *Barcelona Traction* case [1970] ICJ Rep. 3.

time.[65] A number of earlier precedents were invoked but were considered by the ICJ to be exceptions to the rule.[66] Some of this criticism concerned the application by the court of a too rigid standard, "owing to an exaggerated fear of competing claims, thus neglecting the economic realities and leaving the real losers without protection."[67]

The practice at the time did not exclude other choices. The ICJ itself recognized that a state may protect its shareholders in a foreign corporation when their rights were directly infringed, independently from damage inflicted upon the company.[68] The court also considered cases where shareholders may be protected by their state of nationality if the foreign company has ceased to exist or when the state of incorporation lacks the capacity to take action on its behalf.[69] The protection of shareholders who have suffered damage through damage done to the company may also result from an agreement among states.[70]

Recent relevant practice is still more eloquent. In the *Elettronica Sicula* case,[71] the USA brought action before the International Court of Justice against Italy for damage suffered by an Italian company owned by two US companies. In this case the shareholders of the foreign company were protected by their state of nationality against the state of incorporation.[72] In a number of treaties and agreements relating to claims, provision has been made for protection of shareholders in partnerships or companies. For example, a claim was possible by the United Kingdom against Mexico if 50 percent of the total capital was owned by a British subject; this requirement applied respectively for claims by the USA against Peru and Hungary, while a 20 percent share in the total capital was needed for an effective claim by the USA against Yugoslavia.[73] US practice on diplomatic protection also relies on the concept of incorporation and of a share in company ownership by US citizens of at least 50 percent;[74] similarly, Switzerland grants diplomatic

---

[65] For references to the legal literature on the decision see *Oppenheim's International Law*, p. 518, note 4.

[66] García Amador, *The Changing Law*, p. 508.

[67] *Encyclopedia of International Law*, pp. 1053–1054.

[68] See the discussion of the decision in *Oppenheim's International Law*, p. 520.

[69] *Ibid.*, p. 519.

[70] *Encyclopedia of International Law*, p. 1054. See also ICSID Decision on Jurisdiction in *CMS Gas Transmission Co* v. *Argentine Republic*, 17 July 2003, (2003) 42 ILM 788.

[71] *Elettronica Sicula* case [1989] ICJ Rep. 15.

[72] *Oppenheim's International Law*, p. 520; and see generally Foreign Relations Law of the United States, vol. 1, p. 127.

[73] See the discussion of the cases and practice in *Oppenheim's International Law*, pp. 521–522.

[74] *Encyclopedia of International Law*, p. 1053.

protection to a company that is mainly owned by Swiss citizens.[75] The interesting and innovative approach followed in this respect by the Algiers Declaration and in the decisions of the Iran-United States Tribunal, as well as the practice under the International Centre for the Settlement of Investment Disputes, the United Nations Compensation Commission and other arrangements, will be examined further below.

Determining the nationality of corporations is a serious problem when a corporation has a multinational character, which allows a number of states to act on its behalf. This situation is becoming increasingly more common in a globalized economy. International registration of such companies could be helpful in overcoming problems of concurrent nationalities, as is done in respect of trademarks and as has been proposed in respect of a *"societas europaea."*[76]

Although many of these arrangements are based on treaties or special agreements, the aggregate of the practice demonstrates forcefully that the criteria of the *Barcelona Traction* case no longer prevail and that shareholders should be entitled to protection. The theory of corporate personality does not appear any longer to preclude the right to protection of individual shareholders in addition to the criteria that might be followed in respect of the protection of the company as such.

Mass claims settlement and lump sum arrangements: confirming change and adaptation

The greater degree of flexibility in respect of nationality requirements is confirmed by contemporary institutional arrangements for the settlement of mass claims and the practice of lump-sum settlement agreements.

A most relevant source of practice is that of the Iran-United States Claims Tribunal, established to terminate through arbitration "all litigation as between the government of each party and the nationals of the other."[77] For this purpose, a national is defined as a natural person who is a

---

[75] *Ibid.*, p. 1053.
[76] On *"societas europaea"* and its international registration, see the Foreign Relations Law of the United States, vol. 1, p. 131.
[77] Charles N. Brower and Jason D. Brueschke, *The Iran-United States Claims Tribunal* (1998), commenting on the Algiers Claims Settlement Declaration, p. 26, note 104. For the text of the Algiers Declaration and related instruments, see (1981) 20 *International Legal Materials* 230. See also Richard B. Lillich and Daniel B. Magraw (eds.), *The Iran-United States Claims Tribunal: Its Contribution to the Law of State Responsibility* (1998); David D. Caron, "The nature of the Iran-United States Claims Tribunal and the evolving structure of international dispute resolution" 84 *American Journal of International Law* (1990) 104–156.

citizen of either country or a corporation organized under the laws of either party, provided the citizens of the country of incorporation hold, directly or indirectly, a 50 percent interest in its capital stock.[78] In respect of other corporations, however, the Declaration refers to an interest of such nationals enough to control the corporation.[79] The Iran-United States Claims Tribunal considered sufficient for this purpose the ownership by a US company of 49.8 percent of the shares in a corporation organized in Iran.[80]

The first novel solution concerns claims by dual nationals. While such claims are normally excluded from the jurisdiction of tribunals or claims arrangements, the Iran-United States Claims Tribunal has declared the claim admissible if it meets the test of "dominant and effective nationality,"[81] relying for this conclusion on both the *Nottebohm* and the *Mergé* cases.[82] To establish the dominant and effective nationality, the Tribunal has examined the person's "entire life,"[83] with particular reference to the date on which the nationality was acquired, periods of residence in each country, political and social attachments and the integration in each national society.[84] This approach has also been used in respect of the nationality of individuals owning corporate stocks so as to establish whether the 50 percent nationality requirement is met.[85] Although the Iranian judges in the Tribunal have objected to the test, it has been consistently applied.[86]

Another interesting point of innovation concerns the tests applied to corporate entities. The determination of the 50 percent ownership of the capital stock no longer requires elaborate proof, such as certificates of nationality of numerous individuals. Instead, more functional tests have been introduced, such as proxy statements or the record of stockholders with addresses in the USA.[87]

---

[78] Claims Settlement Declaration, Art. VII(1).
[79] See the discussion of these rules in the Foreign Relations Law of the United States, vol. 1, pp. 127–128.
[80] *Sedco Inc. v. National Iranian Oil Co.*, (1987-II) 15 Iran-US Claims Tribunal Reports (Iran-USCTR) 23, as commented on in the Foreign Relations Law of the United States, vol. 1, p. 128.
[81] *Nasser Esphahanian v. Bank Tejarat*, Award No. 522-828-1, 21 October 1991, 27 Iran-USCTR 196. See also Case No. A/18, Decision No. DEC. 32-A18-FT, 6 April 1984, Iran-USCTR 251.
[82] George H. Aldrich, *The Jurisprudence of the Iran-United States Claims Tribunal* (1996), p. 55, with reference to the *Nottebohm* case, [1955] ICJ Rep. 4, and the *Mergé* case, (1955) 14 RIAA 236.
[83] Aldrich, *Jurisprudence*, p. 60.
[84] *Ibid.*, p. 76, and Brower and Brueschke, *Iran-United States Claims Tribunal*, pp. 34–35.
[85] Brower and Brueschke, *Iran-United States Claims Tribunal*, pp. 55–56.
[86] *Ibid.*, pp. 41–42.   [87] *Ibid.*, pp. 47–49.

Jurisdiction has also been extended to non-stock corporations if the ownership meets the test of a 50 percent interest.[88] Partnerships satisfying the 50 percent nationality requirement are also admitted to claim on a *pro rata* basis even if the other partners are prevented from claiming or have not joined the claim.[89] The Tribunal has concluded that "[w]hile international law seems to accept that as a rule a partner may not sue in his own name alone on a cause of action accruing to the partnership, where special reasons or circumstances required it, 'international tribunals have had little difficulty in disaggregating the interests of partners and in permitting' partners to recover their *pro rata* share of partnership claims."[90] In the light of this and other practice, however, one may wonder whether the situation has not changed under general international law itself.

A second relevant source of contemporary practice is that of the United Nations Compensation Commission.[91] While the Commission has not strictly involved an arbitration system, which has been the reason for occasional criticism,[92] the panels convened to decide on the claims apply recognized legal rules and standards of international law.[93] An innovative aspect of the Commission's arrangements relates to the nationality of claimants, where again a greater degree of flexibility has been permitted. For example, under the rules of the Commission, a government may submit claims on behalf of its nationals and "at its discretion, of other persons resident in its territory."[94] The latter evidently concerns not nationals but residents who

---

[88] *Ibid.*, pp. 51–52.

[89] *Ibid.*, pp. 53–55, with reference to *Housing and Urban Services International, Inc.* v. *Government of the Islamic Republic of Iran*, Award No. 201-174-1, 22 November 1985, 9 Iran-USCTR 313.

[90] *Housing and Urban Services International, Inc.* v. *Government of the Islamic Republic of Iran*, Award No. 201-174-1, 22 November 1985, 9 Iran-USCTR 313, at 330, citing D.C. Ohly, "A functional analysis of claimant eligibility" in R.B. Lillich (ed.), *International Law of State Responsibility for Injuries to Aliens* (1983), pp. 281, at 291, as discussed and cited by Brower and Brueschke, *Iran-United States Claims Tribunal*, p. 54.

[91] On the arrangements and the work of the United Nations Compensation Commission, see generally Marci Frigessi di Rattalma, "Le régime de responsabilité internationale institué par le Conseil d'Administration de la Commission de Compensation des Nations Unies" 101 *Revue Générale de Droit International Public* (1997) 45. See also Richard B. Lillich (ed.), *The United Nations Compensation Commission* (1995).

[92] Michael E. Schneider, "How fair and efficient is the United Nations Compensation Commission System?" 15 *Journal of International Arbitration* (1998) 15–26.

[93] See, e.g., the 1999 Report of the F2 Panel, UN Doc. S/AC.26/1999/23 (9 December 1999), para. 14. See also generally Veijo Heiskanen and Robert O'Brien, "UN Compensation Commission Panel sets precedents on government claims" 92 *American Journal of International Law* (1998) 339–350.

[94] United Nations Compensation Commission, Provisional Rules for Claims Procedure, 1992, Art. 5.1.a.

may have the nationality of another state. Trusteeship arrangements are also used to extend protection to persons who are not in a position to have their claims submitted by a government. Under the rules of the Commission, a person, authority or body may be appointed to this effect by the Governing Council.[95]

The rules governing the United Nations Compensation Commission also regulate corporate claims. It should be noted that it is not always the espousal of the state of nationality that is required to submit a claim. Thus, a corporation whose state of incorporation has failed to submit a claim on its behalf, may itself make a claim to the Commission, if it explains why such claim was not submitted by that state.[96] Moreover, if the governments concerned agree, one government may submit claims in respect of joint ventures on behalf of the nationals, corporations or other entities of other governments.[97] Most importantly, shareholders of a corporation who are barred from making a claim because of its nationality may claim for the losses with respect to that corporation.[98] In the case of a partnership which has a separate legal personality and which because of its nationality is ineligible to claim for its losses, each of the eligible partners may claim *pro rata* for the respective proportionate interest.[99] A similar rule applies to partners in a partnership that has no separate legal personality.[100]

The United Nations Compensation Commission has recently taken another innovative step by allowing in some circumstances to reach beyond the traditional limits of the corporate veil. As a general rule, individuals are not allowed to claim for losses suffered by a corporate entity nor to claim in their own right for such losses. But it has happened that a number of claims were made by individuals who had interests in Kuwaiti companies in which they could not appear as owners or shareholders because of domestic nationality requirements in that country. Some of these claims overlapped corporate claims and some stood alone.

Decision 123 (2001) of the Governing Council introduced the rule that due regard should be paid to claims by non-Kuwaiti individuals in circumstances involving losses suffered by Kuwaiti corporate entities.[101] To this end bilateral committees involving Kuwait and a government or entity filing any such claim on behalf of individuals are to be established to make

---

[95] *Ibid.*, Art. 5.2.   [96] *Ibid.*, Art. 5.3.   [97] *Ibid.*, Art. 5.1.b.
[98] United Nations Compensation Commission, Decision of the Governing Council on Business Losses of Individuals, S/AC 26/1991/4, 23 October 1991, para. f.
[99] *Ibid.*, para. d.   [100] *Ibid.*, para. e.
[101] United Nations Compensation Commission, Decision S/AC, 26/Dec. 123 (2001), 15 March 2001.

a determination on the respective entitlement. The United Nations Compensation Commission must implement these determinations, having been given irrevocable authority by Kuwait to distribute payments to successful non-Kuwaiti claimants in these categories. Payments are made on behalf of Kuwait to the intervening governments or claiming entities and are then channelled to the individuals, in amounts as determined by the respective bilateral committee. The bilateral committees consist of three members, one appointed by each party and one appointed as the umpire.

The objectives of the bilateral committees are to "assess and determine a fair and equitable allocation of the compensation, which may in due course be awarded by the Commission in relation to Kuwaiti corporate entities, to claimants in Overlapping Claims or Stand Alone Claims, in such a manner that the allocation, expressed as a percentage share or shares of losses duly claimed, shall be communicated to the Commission and applied by it when disbursing the amounts awarded in due course."[102] The determinations of bilateral committees are final and binding and "shall not be subject to any appeal, review, correction, modification or revision whatsoever, whether at the request of Kuwait or the Adhering State or at the request of a claimant, and regardless of the forum."[103] This novel procedure will allow compensation to reach the rightful claimant beyond the formalities of the corporate veil.

Some scholars have voiced the opinion that these aspects of the practice of the Iran-United States Claims Tribunal or the United Nations Compensation Commission merely represent a *lex specialis* that does not reflect the rules or practice under international law.[104] However, such developments indicate an important degree of evolution in terms of the individual's role in claims settlement and the requirements of jurisdiction.

Furthermore, in a number of respects these developments are confirmed by the recent practice of lump-sum claims settlement. While the admissibility of claims is usually still restricted to nationals, various agreements have

---

[102] United Nations Compensation Commission, Guidelines for the Work of Bilateral Committees to be Formed to Resolve Certain Issues involving the State of Kuwait and Other States relating to Overlapping Claims and Stand Alone Claims at the United Nations Compensation Commission, Annex I, Decision 123.

[103] *Ibid.*, Art. 14.

[104] David J. Bederman, "Lump sum agreements and diplomatic protection," Interim Report prepared for the Committee on Diplomatic Protection of Persons and Property, International Law Association, New Delhi Conference (2002), 3, with reference to Burns H. Weston and Richard B. Lillich, *International Claims: Their Settlement by Lump Sum Agreements* (1975). See also generally Burns H. Weston, Richard B. Lillich and David J. Bederman, *International Claims: Their Settlement by Lump Sum Agreements, 1975–1995* (1999).

given the right to non-nationals to benefit from the claims arrangements.[105] The strict requirement of the past of the rule of continuous nationality has also been relaxed in some contemporary agreements.[106] Again, while claims on behalf of dual nationals are normally excluded, in some arrangements they have been exceptionally admitted.[107] Rules relating to disaggregated partnership claims, as well as those allowing for bringing stockholder claims independently from the corporation, also evidence a substantial change as compared to the traditional standards of diplomatic protection. This again confirms that the restrictive criteria of the *Barcelona Traction* case have been surpassed.[108]

One may conclude that the trends that were becoming evident in the requirements of diplomatic protection have materialized to a meaningful extent in the practice relating to the settlement of mass claims, both in the context of institutionalized arrangements and in that of lump-sum agreements. The dwindling influence of nationality as an element of state control over the claims of individuals under international law evidences the increased recognition of their more complete legal personality. Such recognition is completed by the availability of direct access of individuals and corporations to international courts and tribunals, which will be examined next.

---

[105] Bederman, Draft Report, p. 6.
[106] *Ibid.*, p. 7. [107] *Ibid.*, p. 8. [108] *Ibid.*, pp. 11–12.

4

Individuals before international courts and tribunals: a continuing progression

In the early twentieth century, several remarkable treaties introduced the then novel concept of the direct access of individuals to some international courts and tribunals. This was at the time considered as an exception to the general rule of state exclusivity in international dispute settlement. However, when exception after exception is introduced it is at some point reasonable to ask whether it has not become itself the general rule. Obviously, the answer to this question is not yet positive, but the experience of the twentieth century has clearly established a direction, and it may well be that the evolution will be completed in the present century.

First steps

The first step was to allow an individual to appeal a national decision before an international tribunal. This amounted to a gigantic conceptual innovation in international law, even though restricted to a very specific ambit. This first step was that of the Hague Convention XII of 1907 establishing the International Prize Court, under the terms of which individuals could bring an appeal against the decisions of national prize courts affecting their rights[1] and bring other actions.[2] The effort failed, however, not only because the Convention was never ratified but also for the reason that the state could forbid its nationals from instituting proceedings, or could do

---

[1] P.K. Menon, "The subjects of modern international law" 3 *Hague Yearbook of International Law* (1990) 30–86, at 65–66.
[2] Marek St. Korowicz, "The problem of the international personality of individuals" 50 *American Journal of International Law* (1956) 533–562, at 545–546.

so in lieu of the individual,[3] which showed that the state still prevailed in the claim process.

The second step in this evolution allowed for direct standing of individuals before an international tribunal who could bring claims against states. This was the case of the Central American Court of Justice, created in 1907 and discontinued in 1918 after a ten-year period.[4] This experience was conceptually more successful in that the individual could bring actions against any of the Central American states parties except that of his or her own nationality, and could do so irrespective of whether his or her national government supported the claim. Exhaustion of local remedies or the evidence of denial of justice were important requirements for the admissibility of the claim. In the above period, four claims failed on admissibility grounds and in one other the claimant failed on the merits. The practice was therefore not entirely successful but the precedent was nonetheless significant. It should be recalled that this group of states constituted a closely knit community, given their common historical experience, thereby facilitating the establishment of common institutions, not unlike what is today the experience of the European Community.

The third step also allowed for individuals to bring claims against a foreign state before an international tribunal, but more in the line of mass claims for war damage. The Treaty of Versailles allowed nationals of the Allied and associated powers to bring claims against Germany before Mixed Arbitral Tribunals, while other peace treaties of the time allowed for claims by individuals against nationals or governments of the defeated states.[5] While occasionally the international character of these tribunals has been questioned,[6] their jurisprudence clearly marked both their international nature and their role in respect of the individual. In fact, the right to compensation of individuals as nationals was recognized, quite separately from the discretion of the governments,[7] as was their right to claim independently of the intervention of their governments on the one occasion where this right was questioned.[8] In addition, the Treaty of Versailles made the

---

[3] *Ibid.*

[4] Menon, "Subjects," 64–65; Korowicz, "International personality," 546.

[5] Menon, "Subjects," 66.

[6] For a discussion of the legal nature of the Mixed Arbitral Tribunals, see Korowicz, "International personality," 546–547.

[7] *Lederer* v. *German Government*, Anglo-German Mixed Arbitral Tribunal (1924) Recueil des Decisions des Tribunaux Arbitraux Mixtes 762, at 768, as cited by Menon, "Subjects," 66, note 136.

[8] *Sigwald, Charles* v. *Germany*, French-German Mixed Arbitral Tribunal, Case No. 255, as cited by Menon, "Subjects," 66, note 137.

well-known contribution to the tripartite representation before the International Labor Organization,[9] and provided for the responsibility of certain individuals for war crimes.[10]

The possibility of claiming against the state of the individual's nationality before an international tribunal was another significant step in this sequence. This was provided for, rather unexpectedly, by the German-Polish Upper Silesian Convention of 1922.[11] While the Convention allowed for claims by individuals against the state in order to protect acquired rights, it did not specify precisely which state was to be the defendant.[12] The question whether a claimant could sue his own state before an arbitral tribunal arose in a case in 1927,[13] and was answered favorably by the tribunal.

Similarly, the Convention, following the League of Nations policy, provided for the protection of minorities. Individuals could make petitions to the national Minorities Office, request an opinion from the President of the Mixed Commission and, if unsuccessful, appeal to the Council of the League of Nations. The rules of procedure of the Mixed Commission went beyond the request for a mere opinion and gave the petitioner the status of a party litigating against the National Minorities Office that represented the national authorities.[14] Again, the right of individuals to bring an action against their respective state before an international tribunal was recognized.

The problem of the right of individuals to petition an international body arose in the context of the regime relating to the protection of minorities established under the League of Nations and related conventions. However, this was concerned more with the recognition of rights than with judicial mechanisms for their enforcement, thus granting individuals a limited capacity to make petitions, without becoming full participants in international procedures.[15] The rights of individuals under treaties were to a significant degree recognized at the time by the Permanent Court of International Justice.[16] The right to petition by minorities and other groups was carried over under the Charter of the United Nations in the specific context

---

[9] Korowicz, "International personality," 547.   [10] *Ibid.*, 546.   [11] *Ibid.*, 552–558.

[12] German-Polish Upper Silesian Convention, 15 May 1922, Art. 5.

[13] *Steiner and Gross* v. *Poland*, Upper Silesian Arbitral Tribunal, Decision of 30 March 1929, as referred to by Korowicz, "International personality," 554.

[14] Korowicz, "International personality," 555–557.   [15] *Ibid.*, 554–555.

[16] *Case Concerning the Jurisdiction of the Courts of Danzig*, Permanent Court of International Justice, Advisory Opinion No. 15, Ser. B, 17–21, and discussion by Menon, "Subjects," 69–70.

of the Trusteeship Council and, later, in the context of the protection of human rights.[17]

Limited international procedures were also made available to individuals, both as claimants and defendants, before the Supreme Restitution Council established in 1952 for claims relating to the restitution of property in connection with the Second World War.[18] Creditors and debtors could also bring their disputes to the Mixed Commission created by the Agreement on German External Debts in 1953.[19]

Limited as this early experience was, it nevertheless contained all the relevant conceptual elements that served as the basis for the massive developments that would take place in the second half of the twentieth century. These developments relate to the recognition of the legal personality of individuals to sue or be sued before international tribunals.

Human rights at the forefront of the individual's international legal personality

The central place assigned to the individual in the Charter of the United Nations opened an entirely new phase in the recognition of substantive human rights and in the procedures for implementing and enforcing such rights. Sir Hersch Lauterpacht wrote in this connection:

As a result of the Charter of the United Nations – as well as of other changes in international law – the individual has acquired a status and a stature which have transformed him from the object of international compassion into a subject of international rights. For in so far as international law is embodied in the Charter, and elsewhere recognizes fundamental rights of the individual independent of the law of the State, to that extent it constitutes the individual as subject of the law of nations.[20]

Although this is not the occasion to discuss human rights developments, it must be emphasized that the Charter has made a significant contribution in respect of the international legal personality of the individual. The international mechanisms set up under the United Nations have provided for

---

[17] Rosalyn Higgins, "Conceptual thinking about the individual in international law" in Falk, Kratochwil and Mendlovitz (eds.), *International Law: A Contemporary Perspective* (1985), pp. 476–494, at 481.

[18] Menon, "Subjects," 68.   [19] *Ibid.*

[20] Sir Hersch Lauterpacht, *International Law and Human Rights* (1950), p. 4, and discussion by Korowicz, "International personality," 549.

broad access of individuals to the enforcement of the rights recognized in various treaties and other instruments.[21] In particular, one should mention the Human Rights Commission and the Committees entrusted with the work of the Covenant and other specialized conventions. Parallel regional developments have resulted in the European and the American Conventions on Human Rights.

The access of the individual to international mechanisms ranges from the more traditional right of petition to complaints before investigating bodies and includes bringing cases before judicial bodies, as an alternative. This can be done directly, as in the European Court of Human Rights, or indirectly, through the intervention of the Commission under the Inter-American Court of Human Rights. What is more important is the availability of these mechanisms either in global terms or in broad regional scales, which is a significant difference when compared to early treaty regimes that covered only limited groups of people, geographical areas or specialized subjects.

In spite of this important progress, Cassese has noted that except where the right of the individual has been recognized to litigate before an international court, the mechanisms provided are mainly concerned with procedural rights. The object of such procedural arrangements is to establish a violation of rights on the part of the defendant state, but then the remedy or compensation is largely left in the hands of the very same state.[22] Such access to international bodies is allowed only under specific treaties, and even then it is not always accepted by all the states parties to the treaties.[23] Cassese notes further that this procedure is concerned more with control rather than with a full judicial process involving the complete range of remedies.[24]

Although one must admit these shortcomings, it is nonetheless remarkable that states have accepted to be accountable before international bodies in respect of the observance of human rights and related rules of international law, this being so as a result of action brought by their own nationals.[25] Perhaps still more remarkable is the high degree of compliance by states with the decisions rendered in such matters.[26]

The developments taking place in the law of human rights further reinforce the conclusion that, in a number of areas, nationality is becoming less and less significant in terms of the protection of the rights of the individual. However, the argument has also been made that the protection of human

---

[21] Menon, "Subjects," 73–79.

[22] Antonio Cassese, "Les individus" in Mohammed Bedjaoui (rédacteur général), *Droit International. Bilan et Perspectives* (1991), pp. 119–127, at 124.

[23] *Ibid.*, p. 124.   [24] *Ibid.*, p. 125.   [25] *Ibid.*, p. 125.   [26] *Ibid.*, p. 126.

rights is a special field, as compared with situations where diplomatic protection is exercised, or with mechanisms of investment protection.[27] It is thought in this context that diplomatic protection should be maintained to safeguard the economic interests of individuals.

While, historically, diplomatic protection has encompassed both the economic interests and the treatment of individuals abroad, the law of human rights has evolved beyond the framework of traditional diplomatic protection, following more liberal rules and allowing more readily for claims against the state of nationality. The same path is followed in other areas of the law typically relating to economic interests, such as the law of investments. This shows that the evolution is not so much related to the nature of the rights but to the role of the individual in the international legal system. Furthermore, economic rights are considered today to be a part of human rights, thus also justifying liberal mechanisms of protection. Naturally, this does not mean that in different areas of law different rules and requirements might not be followed as to the protection of rights of individuals. However, the underlying premise will always be the same, that is, the assertion of the rights of the individual as such.

There can be little doubt that the twenty-first century will witness an important completion of the framework for the protection of the rights of the individual, with the intervention of international institutions and the participation therein of the affected or interested individuals. The scope of the international legal personality of such individuals will thus be further broadened.

However, a note of caution must also be sounded. The evolution will progress so long as it responds to the genuine purpose of enhancing the rights of the individual, as has been the case in most of the evolution so far, and to this end the cooperation and participation of states is also encouraged. But in a number of instances the issue of human rights appears to have been used for purposes other than that genuine concern. This leads to the politicization of the discussion and to the alienation of the states, to the point efforts in this direction will be perceived not as benefiting the individual but as an instrument for antagonizing a particular policy or government. If it persists, this distortion of the law of human rights will mean a step backwards, not forwards, particularly if it results in condemning violations of human rights by some governments and condoning those of other governments on grounds of political affinity.

---

[27] Orrego Vicuña, ILA Report, pp. 631–647. See also comments by Bilder and Cerar in the Report.

International humanitarian law and the law of warfare: individual responsibility under international law

The enjoyment of rights and their safeguard is only one aspect of the international legal personality of individuals under international law. The other aspect is the recognition of duties and the direct responsibility for their infringement. In this field as well there was a constant progress of international law in the past century, which will certainly achieve a greater development in the twenty-first century.

Although Part VII of the Treaty of Versailles had already made explicit this kind of individual responsibility for war crimes and had established an international tribunal for this purpose,[28] it would be for the Nürnberg Tribunal to issue the following statement:

It was submitted that international law is concerned with the actions of sovereign States, and provides no punishment for individuals; and further, that where the act in question is an act of State, those who carry it out are not personally responsible but are protected by the doctrine of the sovereignty of the State. In the opinion of the Tribunal, both these submissions must be rejected. That international law imposes duties and liabilities upon individuals as well as upon States has long been recognized.[29]

Since the recognition of these principles by the United Nations General Assembly Resolution 95(I) of 11 December 1946,[30] this has become an established doctrine. This is particularly visible in the work of the United Nations, and has inspired a number of other conventions on the laws of war, most notably the 1949 Geneva Conventions on Treatment of Prisoners of War and Protection of Civilian Persons in Time of War.[31]

Parallel developments in the prohibition of piracy, the nationality of ships, the crime of genocide and a number of other matters defined as crimes under international law have engaged the direct responsibility of individuals,[32] thus confirming the prevailing trend.

The establishment of an International Criminal Court had also been proposed a long time ago. A Committee of Jurists appointed by the Council of the League of Nations in 1934, prepared several conventions responding to

---

[28] Korowicz, "International personality," 546.
[29] International Military Tribunal for the Trial of Major German War Criminals, Judgment 30 September 1946 (Cmd. 6964), pp. 41–42, and discussion by Korowicz, "International personality," 550, and by Menon, "Subjects," 81.
[30] Menon, "Subjects," 81–82.   [31] *Ibid.*, 81–82.   [32] *Ibid.*, 79–83.

concerns raised by a number of acts of international terrorism. One of those proposals concerned an International Penal Court before which individuals could be accused and individual claims for damages brought.[33] However, it was not until the end of the century that two related developments began to give substance to these efforts: the establishment of the International Tribunals for Yugoslavia and for Rwanda, as well as the creation of an International Criminal Court.

The first of these international tribunals was established for the purpose of prosecuting persons responsible for serious violations of international humanitarian law committed in the territory of the former Yugoslavia.[34] A similar international tribunal was established for the prosecution of persons responsible for genocide and other serious violations of international humanitarian law committed in the territory of Rwanda, or by Rwandan citizens in neighboring states.[35]

While broadly opening the way for the prosecution and punishment of individuals responsible for crimes against humanity, whether related to conflicts or not, and thus helping to clarify the law in this respect, these tribunals have developed a number of questionable practices and interpretations. From a material point of view, the extremely broad definition of crimes against humanity adopted appears to encompass activities that might not normally have qualified as such. From the point of view of due process and the very protection of the human rights of the accused, even more troubling is the practice of issuing secret indictments and hearing anonymous witnesses. Nor has the risk of political utilization of the tribunal by governments and officials helped to convey the necessary image of impartiality and balance that an institution of this kind needs to ensure, particularly in the aftermath of the events in Kosovo.

A more elaborate effort was the creation of the International Criminal Court (ICC), the statute of which was adopted by the United Nations Diplomatic Conference in Rome on 17 July 1998.[36] This is yet another important development and clarification of the law in establishing the responsibility of individuals for the crime of genocide, crimes against humanity, war crimes

---

[33] League of Nations doc. V. C. 94, M. 47, 1938, as cited by Edvard I. Hambro, "Individuals before international tribunals" in *Proceedings of the American Society of International Law* (1941), pp. 22–29, at 24–25.

[34] Security Council Resolution 827 (1993), 25 May 1993.

[35] Security Council Resolution 955 (1994), 8 November 1994.

[36] Doc. A/CONF 183/9. For the text of the Statute see (1998) 37 *International Legal Materials* 999. The Statute entered into force on 1 July 2002.

and aggression.[37] The jurisdiction of the ICC is qualified in a variety of ways, generally reflecting the emphasis placed by governments on the priority accorded to national jurisdiction and existing treaty obligations.[38] Further definition has been added to the crimes within the jurisdiction of the ICC in the Elements of Crimes, adopted by the Preparatory Commission for the International Criminal Court on 30 June 2000.[39]

An important feature of the ICC is that its jurisdiction is "complementary" to national criminal jurisdiction. National investigation and prosecution of crimes over which the ICC has jurisdiction is the rule. However, the ICC may exercise jurisdiction over such crimes if it determines that a national judicial system is "unwilling or unable" to carry out investigation or prosecution, or has collapsed. This approach is different from that of the International Criminal Tribunals for the Former Yugoslavia and Rwanda, whose jurisdictions are concurrent with those of national courts but which are accorded priority, in that the tribunals may request the latter to defer to their competence.

Notwithstanding the various qualifications of the jurisdiction of the ICC, a number of aspects would require clarification so as to meet the concerns of many countries, including not only major powers but also developing nations. The following problems requiring clarification can be mentioned: the broad powers of the Prosecutor to initiate action, even *proprio motu*; the difficult structural relationship with the Security Council; the not very precise guarantee of non-retroactivity in view of conflicting interpretations about certain types of crimes in this respect; the potential distortion of the above-mentioned principle of complementarity which could lead the ICC

---

[37] See, e.g., G. Sluiter, "An International Criminal Court is hereby established" 16 *Netherlands Quarterly of Human Rights* (1998) 413–420; B.S. Brown, "Primacy and complementarity: reconciling the jurisdiction of national courts and international criminal tribunals" 23 *Yale Journal of International Law* (1998) 384–436; papers presented at a symposium on "The International Criminal Court: a critical review of the results of the Rome Conference," convened in honor of Judge Antonio Cassese, Erasmus University, Rotterdam, 5 November 1998.

[38] See the discussion of this and other tribunals in Francisco Orrego Vicuña and Christopher Pinto, *The Peaceful Settlement of Disputes: Prospects for the Twenty-first Century*, Final Report for the Centennial Commemoration of the First Peace Conference, May 1999, published in F. Kalhoven (ed.), *The Centennial of the First Peace Conference* (2000), p. 388. See also Alfred P. Rubin, "Challenging the conventional wisdom: another view of the International Criminal Court" 52 *Journal of International Affairs* (1999) 783–794; and M. Cherif Bassiouni, "Policy perspectives favoring the establishment of the International Criminal Court" 52 *Journal of International Affairs* (1999) 795–810.

[39] Report of the Preparatory Commission for the International Criminal Court, Addendum, Part II: Finalized Draft Text of the Elements of Crimes, UN Doc. PCNICC/2000/1/Add.2.

to ignore the ability or willingness of a country to prosecute; and a number of constitutional issues that arise in various countries about the role of the judiciary.

Not less troubling is what seems to be the endless expansion of the concept of crimes against humanity in some decisions of national and international courts, often on feeble grounds. Apart from specific legal issues one can also detect the shadow of the intention of political utilization of the ICC. The combination of governmental influences with actions by non-governmental organizations active in the field could lead to a situation where political antagonisms might substitute for the genuine humanitarian concern rightly inspiring the establishment of the ICC. This is particularly troublesome for developing countries and for others engaged in bitter historical regional conflicts. Should this be the case, not progress but regression would ensue, setting back the cause of human rights more generally.

Specialized courts and tribunals

Recognition of the international legal personality of the individual in terms of granting direct access to dispute settlement mechanisms is also a frequent feature of specialized courts and tribunals in the field of trade, investments and other areas of international activity. In some of these areas, where participating states have very close relations, the arrangements transcend the sphere of pure international law towards a quasi-federal system of law. An example is the Court of Justice of the European Community (ECJ). In view of their specialized nature, the most significant of these arrangements will be examined in a separate chapter.

Should individuals acquire standing before the International Court of Justice?

Most of the arrangements examined above, like those that will be examined in the next chapter, have dealt with courts or tribunals intervening in specific areas of the law or in particular circumstances. A further question is whether individuals, corporations and other legal entities might be granted similar access to courts dealing with the settlement of disputes in a broader context, such as international law generally, of which the International Court of Justice is the best example.

The question was considered by the Committee of Jurists appointed by the League of Nations to prepare the Statute of the Permanent Court of International Justice. At that time, Lord Phillimore pronounced his famous but perhaps short-sighted *dictum* that "a State would never permit itself to be sued before a court by a private individual."[40] The Statute of the Court provided that "only States may be parties in cases before the Court."[41]

This approach was challenged in the Committee by Professors Loder and De Lapradelle,[42] and as mentioned above it did not survive the test of history. States did eventually accept to be sued by individuals before international courts in some cases. Already in 1923, the Institut de Droit International recommended granting international organizations the right to sue before the Permanent Court of International Justice. In 1929 it addressed the rights of persons and recommended that individuals be granted access to international tribunals in some cases.[43]

It would be again Sir Hersch Lauterpacht who put the issue in the right perspective. He pointed out that the importance of the provision of Article 34(1) of the Statute should not be exaggerated as it only defines the competence of the court and it is "not intended to be declaratory of any general principle of international law."[44] The individual might not have access to this particular court, nor to other inter-state dispute settlement arrangements, but there is nothing in the system of international law as conceived today that constitutes a bar to this possibility.

As Rosenne has explained, a number of cases before the ICJ have been intimately concerned with the protection of the individual and corporations, but it has always been the state that acts on behalf of that interest. Notable cases in this category have included *Anglo-Iranian Oil Co.; Asylum; Haya de la Torre; Ambatielos; Nottebohm* and *Barcelona Traction.*[45] Rosenne rightly concludes that "[i]t is possible that the direct representation of the individuals concerned in the proceedings before the Court would have the effect not only of stimulating public interest in the work of the Court but also, and this may be more important, of enhancing its prestige and public confidence in the reality of international justice."[46]

---

[40] Korowicz, "International personality," 543–544, 560–561.

[41] Statute of the International Court of Justice, Art. 34(1).

[42] See the discussion by Menon, "Subjects," 64, note 131.

[43] Hambro, "Individuals" 25, with reference to the work of the Institut de Droit International. See also generally F. von der Heydte, "L'individu et les tribunaux internationaux" III *Recueil des Cours de l'Academie de Droit International* (1962) 287–358.

[44] Lauterpacht, *International Law*, p. 48, and discussion of this and other views of Sir Hersch in Shabtai Rosenne, *The Law and Practice of the International Court, 1920–1996* (1997), p. 655.

[45] *Ibid.*, p. 654 with references to these and other cases.

[46] *Ibid.*, p. 655. See also generally Nicholas Poulantzas, "The individual before international jurisdiction" 15 *Revue Héllenique de Droit International* (1962) 375–390.

Although it is the state and the government that are the *dominus litis* in proceedings before the ICJ,[47] it has been suggested that individuals could participate in contentious proceedings and present their own case with the assistance of the states parties.[48] In a number of cases the parties have put forth documents and viewpoints of private parties in their pleadings and there seems to be no obstacle for the individual to do so directly. This is particularly the case when the ICJ has to undertake investigative functions or find out about the motives of individuals, as in the *Nottebohm* case.[49] In another case, however, the ICJ appears to have deliberately declined to have information provided by an infant. The court even changed the early title from *Case concerning the Guardianship of an Infant* to *Application of the Convention of 1902 Governing the Guardianship of Infants*, so as to focus on the issue of treaty interpretation.[50]

This kind of development does not appear to need an amendment of the Statute, for it is not inconsistent with Article 34. Rosenne has written in this respect that:

in appropriate cases the International Court of Justice should take advantage of all the powers which it already possesses, and permit an individual directly concerned to present himself before the Court, or before some appropriate body (such as the Chamber of Summary Procedure) and give his own version of the facts and his own construction of the law. It is not believed that is inevitably excluded, either by the language of Article 34 of the Statute, or by the essential judicial character of the contentious jurisdiction applicable only between States.[51]

Proposals have also been made to authorize individuals and non-governmental organizations to request advisory opinions from the International Court of Justice,[52] following the precedent of international organizations. In this respect, however, as noted earlier,[53] there is a serious

---

[47] Shabtai Rosenne, "Reflections on the position of the individual in inter-state litigation in the International Court of Justice" in *International Arbitration, Liber Amicorum for Martin Domke* (1967), pp. 240–251, reprinted in Rosenne, *An International Law Miscellany* (1993), ch. 2, p. 112.

[48] Shabtai Rosenne, "Lessons of the past and needs of the future" in Connie Peck and Roy S. Lee (eds.), *Increasing the Effectiveness of the International Court of Justice* (1997), pp. 466–492, at 487–488.

[49] Rosenne, *Miscellany*, pp. 113–114, with reference to *Nottebohm* and other cases.

[50] Rosenne, *Miscellany*, p. 114.

[51] *Ibid.*, p. 123.

[52] See, e.g., M.C.W. Pinto, "The Court and other international tribunals" in Peck and Lee, *Increasing the Effectiveness*, pp. 281–309, at 285.

[53] See chapter 2, note 66 and associated text.

concern about the risk of introducing heavily politicized issues within the ambit of the ICJ or else of distorting the nature of the judicial system. This option might be justified in the future to the extent that the role of such entities in the international community is clearly established and they satisfy accepted standards of professionalism, accountability and transparency.

It may be useful to keep in mind, in the context of access to the advisory functions of the ICJ, the distinction affecting the status of observer made in the Antarctic Treaty System between non-governmental organizations of a scientific or professional character and those engaged in activities of a political nature. To a limited extent this innovation in the functions of the ICJ could also be accommodated without a formal amendment of the Statute.

If the role of the individual in international dispute settlement is examined in the broad perspective of the evolution of international law it is not difficult to agree with Judge Higgins who writes that "there are powerful arguments for giving him access – through a revision of its Statute – to the International Court or perhaps to a special Chamber of that Court."[54] Although the revision of the Statute would be a difficult political exercise, the states parties might in any event wish to consider this alternative at some point in time. The role of the ICJ in the international community is inextricably related to this step.[55]

Judge Higgins has also pointed to the need to accompany this development with an efficient screening service to sift misconceived or frivolous claims, somewhat along the lines of the former practice of the European Commission of Human Rights which would declare claims to be admissible or inadmissible at a preliminary stage, a function exercised now by the European Court of Human Rights.[56] It was earlier suggested that a high level Special Committee of Jurists might be established to work with the ICJ in this respect, particularly in terms of advising and reporting on the requests for advisory opinions by international organizations, individuals and other entities.[57] This Committee might also provide a screening service for the purpose of claims by individuals and other entities before the ICJ if these were allowed.

---

[54] Higgins, "Conceptual thinking," 476–494, 481.
[55] See the discussion in this respect of Orrego Vicuña and Pinto, Report, 1999.
[56] Higgins, "Conceptual thinking," 482.
[57] See chapter 2, note 72 and associated text.

Claims before domestic courts and restrictive approaches to sovereign immunity

It has been pointed out that a foreign national is often allowed to bring claims before the courts of the defendant state or even in respect of claims against third states. This policy has been encouraged by the OECD with particular reference to the need not to discriminate between nationals and foreigners in this respect.[58] Some states allow recovery by foreign claimants subject to reciprocity,[59] but eventually this condition should be abandoned with respect to foreign private claimants. While this type of action is domestic in terms of the forum chosen, it is also international in terms of the legal issues and the litigants involved, and of course it opens up a very large role for national courts in the application and interpretation of international law.

The settlement of disputes before national courts is not devoid of serious difficulties. First, there is a risk of inconsistency in decisions of courts as they respond to many different legal systems, a situation that may end up affecting the implementation of international agreements and their interpretation. Referral of questions on interpretation of international law to international courts may provide an adequate solution to this problem, as evidenced by the experience of the ECJ. A similar mechanism suggested for the International Court of Justice would involve referral by both high domestic courts and other international tribunals.[60] A question of impartiality may also arise when courts must pass judgment on entities that have the same national allegiance as the court or on the state itself.

The intervention of domestic courts also involves important issues of conflict of law. Because of the existence of a multi-jurisdictional basis, the establishment of personal jurisdiction will often not be an easy task. Questions related to the place where damage has been done, where the defendant has its domicile or conducted business, the degree of minimum contact considered necessary, the influence of the doctrine of *forum non conveniens* where accepted, and other such issues, have been clearly illustrated by leading cases. *Bhopal*,[61] *Amoco Cadiz*,[62] *Mines de Potasse d'Alsace*[63] and many

---

[58] See chapter 3, note 33 and associated text.
[59] See e.g., the United States Oil Pollution Act 1990, s. 2707.
[60] See Art. 177 of the Treaty establishing the European Economic Community, and chapter 2, notes 69, 70 and associated text.
[61] *In Re Union Carbide Corp. Gas Plant Disaster*, 809 F 2d 195 (2nd Cir. 1987).
[62] *In Re Oil Spill of "Amoco Cadiz,"* 699 F 2d 909 (17th Cir. 1983).
[63] *Bier* v. *Mines de Potasse d'Alsace* [1976] ECR 1735.

others are eloquent in this respect. Questions of concurrent jurisdiction and forum-shopping should also be taken into account in this context in order to prevent abuse by potential claimants.

As noted by Judge Higgins, the difficulty here does not relate so much to the access of the individual to the court but to bringing the other party before such court, particularly if it is a foreign state or government that might plead sovereign immunity.[64] This traditional bar to the exercise of jurisdiction by domestic courts has been, however, gradually eroded. Immunity has been excluded from commercial transactions and other acts *jure gestionis*: the conferral of immunity in such cases has often resulted in leaving the individual unprotected under international law when trade, investment or economic activities are involved. A functional test directed at identifying the nature of the activity involved, as opposed to the status of the trader, has been developed better to ensure this protection to individuals. An important application of this concept in a recent ICSID decision will be discussed below.

Notwithstanding the important development of international jurisdictions granting direct access to individuals, domestic courts will retain a meaningful role in dispute settlement. The exhaustion of local remedies is still a central principle of international law that must normally be complied with before international action is taken.[65] A measure of flexibility has also been introduced in this context but it relates more to the issue of denial of justice or lack of remedies than to the weakening of the principle as such.[66]

[64] Higgins, "Conceptual thinking," 482–483.

[65] Juliane Kokott, *The Exhaustion of Local Remedies*, Interim Report prepared for the Committee on Diplomatic Protection of Persons and Property, International Law Association, Sixty-Ninth Conference (2000), pp. 606–630.

[66] *Ibid.*, pp. 621–625.

5

Shaping a new role for the individual in international dispute settlement: the contribution of specialized jurisdictions

Emerging trends in a global society

It has been pointed out above that the current process of economic globalization is having a potentially decisive impact on the structure of international society and the evolving role of international law. A particular expression of this development is the prominent role assumed by the individual in international dispute settlement related to such globalization. This role has already been well established in the context of investment disputes and is beginning to permeate the arrangements for dispute settlement in international trade, economic integration and other specialized forms of jurisdiction, the most relevant of which will be examined in this chapter.

A highly influential factor in this process is the role of market economies in the context of globalization, which constitutes a common thread underlying most of the new dispute settlement arrangements. As Shihata has explained with regard to national dispute settlement arrangements:

The settlement of disputes through adequate institutions acquires a unique importance in the context of transition from a command economy to a market economy. In the former, the function of dispute-settlement institutions is perhaps akin to an administrative one, mostly concerned with the timely fulfillment of an economic plan. In a market economy, by contrast, economic actors will be left, within certain limits defined by law, to pursue their own economic strategies. Long-term success of those strategies will depend on a climate of stability and predictability, where business risks may be rationally assessed, transaction costs lowered, market failures addressed and governmental arbitrariness reduced. In such a context, fair and efficient dispute settlement institutions will be required as an integral part of the legal framework.[1]

---

[1] Ibrahim F.I. Shihata, *Complementary Reform: Essays on Legal, Judicial and Other Institutional Reforms Supported by the World Bank* (1998), pp. 33–34.

These remarks are still more pertinent in respect of international dispute settlement, where the global market is many times more uncertain and less predictable than a national legal environment and hence there is a higher risk for investments, trade and other business undertakings. Adequate dispute settlement arrangements are crucial for creating a business climate conducive to encourage such transactions.

It must also be pointed out that in a competitive environment of this kind rules and contracts are normally observed not so much as a result of the availability of enforcement mechanisms but in order to preserve a reputation and avoid adverse business consequences.[2] Formal dispute settlement will normally be used as a mechanism of last resort and other alternatives will be pursued if available,[3] thus contributing to the development of alternative dispute resolution mechanisms. These other alternatives will be discussed in chapter 7.

The individual as a claimant in its own right: ICSID's turning point

The most significant contemporary step in providing direct access of individuals to international dispute settlement procedures was provided by the 1965 Convention on the Settlement of Investment Disputes between States and Nationals of Other States. The International Centre for Settlement of Investment Disputes (ICSID) was established under this Convention with the sponsorship of the World Bank.[4] This initiative was specifically aimed at making available arbitration and conciliation procedures to foreign investors and in so doing to avoid the traditional recourse to diplomatic protection. The latter is excluded under the Convention to the extent that there is consent to arbitration and compliance with the award.[5] The Convention thus constituted a key turning point in international dispute settlement, signaling the minimization of state intervention involved in

---

[2] *Ibid.*, p. 34.

[3] *Ibid.*, pp. 34–35. See also generally Angela Del Vecchio, *Giurisdizione Internazionale e Globalizzazione* (2003); Laurence Boisson de Chazournes, "Mondialisation et règlement des différends: defis et reponses" 4 *International Law Forum* (2002) 26–31.

[4] Ibrahim F.I. Shihata and Antonio R. Parra, "The experience of the International Centre for Settlement of Investment Disputes" 14 *ICSID Review-Foreign Investment Law Journal* (1999) 299–361.

[5] Convention on the Settlement of Investment Disputes between States and Nationals of Other States, 18 March 1965, 575 UNTS 159, Art. 27 (hereinafter cited as ICSID Convention).

diplomatic protection and highlighting the individual's own role in acceding to such arrangements.

ICSID's central jurisdictional task is to decide disputes between private investors and states;[6] it has no jurisdiction to arbitrate disputes between two states or between two private entities. Notwithstanding this central role of the individual and the state, neither the term "national of another Contracting State" nor the term "Contracting State" is defined in the Convention. The Convention does outline some elements in respect of the standing of a constituent subdivision or agency of a contracting state and the modalities of consent in their respect.[7] It also reflects the concept of control of a company. Under Article 25(2)(b) a juridical person which has the nationality of the contracting state to the dispute may be a party to the proceedings if, because of foreign control, the parties have agreed that the juridical person should be treated as a national of another contracting state.[8] The practice and jurisprudence of ICSID have, however, helped to clarify the meaning of these terms.[9] For example, in the case of *Ceskoslovenska Obchodni Banka, A. S. v. Slovak Republic*, an ICSID tribunal applied a functional test to the determination of who is to be considered a national of a contracting state.[10] The tribunal held that state ownership of the shares of a corporate entity did not preclude such entity from bringing a claim under the Convention as a national of a contracting state, so long as the activities themselves were "essentially commercial rather than governmental in nature."[11]

This approach suggests that the concept of a national of a contracting state may include public entities to the extent they perform private functions, just as a private entity established to perform public functions could be considered as a state entity under the Convention. An analogous situation was considered at the time of the drafting of the Convention. As explained by a leading authority, it would seem that "a mixed economy company or

---

[6] Aron Broches, "The Convention on the Settlement of Investment Disputes: some observations on jurisdiction" 5 *Columbia Journal of International Law* (1966) 263, at 265. See also Elihu Lauterpacht "The World Bank Convention on the Settlement of International Investment Disputes" in *Recueil d'études de droit international en hommage à Paul Guggenheim* (1968), pp. 642–664.

[7] ICSID Convention, Art. 25(1), (3). See C. Schreuer, "Commentary on the ICSID Convention. Article 25", 11 *ICSID Review–Foreign Investment Law Journal* (1996) 318, at 380–391. See also generally C. Schreuer, *The ICSID Convention: A Commentary* (2001).

[8] ICSID Convention, Art. 25.2.b.

[9] On ICSID practice, see generally Schreuer, *The ICSID Convention*.

[10] *Ceskoslovenska Obchodni Banka, A.S. v. Slovak Republic*, ICSID Case No. ARB/97/4, Decision on Objections to Jurisdiction, 24 May 1999, 14 *ICSID Review–Foreign Investment Law Journal* (1999) 250.

[11] *Ibid.*, para. 20.

government-owned corporation should not be disqualified as a 'national of another Contracting State' unless it is acting as an agent for the government or is discharging an essentially governmental function."[12]

ICSID's jurisdiction is based exclusively on the acceptance by both parties to submit to it disputes,[13] giving rise to an impressive number of bilateral and multilateral treaties, legislation and contracts where such consent is expressed. Over 2,000 treaties of this kind are in force.[14] Normally, consent to arbitration is given by a state in anticipation of a dispute, but individuals need not agree until the moment when they bring a claim to ICSID.[15] Although this situation has occasionally been considered as an example of arbitration without privity,[16] it is in fact a form of consent given at different points in time. The role of ICSID has been further expanded by means of the intervention of the Additional Facility, which allows for the participation, in limited circumstances, of parties that are neither a contracting state nor a national of a contracting state.[17]

That the ICSID mechanism is one of fully internationalized arbitration is further supported by the insulation of the proceedings from the control of national courts, as the consent to arbitration is to the exclusion of any other remedy.[18] The exhaustion of local remedies, however, may be required by the contracting state as a condition of its consent to arbitration.[19] This evidences that the principle requiring such exhaustion remains in force and it is compatible with the development of international arbitration.[20] Awards are enforced by contracting states with the same authority as if they were a final judgment of a court in that state.[21]

Other aspects of ICSID practice and jurisprudence also have a direct connection with the globalization of foreign investments and the role of

[12] Aron Broches, "The Convention on the Settlement of Investment Disputes Between States and Nationals of Other States" in *Recueil des Cours de l'Academie de Droit International* (1972), p. 355. A distinction between a government agency performing public functions and also a role typical of private entities was made so as to establish responsibility in *Emilio Agustin Maffezini* v. *Kingdom of Spain*, ICSID Case No. ARB/97/7, Award of 13 November 2000, in www.worldbank.org/icsid/cases/awards.htm

[13] Shihata and Parra, "Experience of ICSID," 302–306.

[14] Antonio R. Parra, "Provisions on the settlement of investment disputes in modern investment laws, bilateral investment treaties and multilateral instruments on investment" 12 *ICSID Review–Foreign Investment Law Journal* (1997) 287–364.

[15] Shihata and Parra, "Experience of ICSID," 304.

[16] J. Paulsson, "Arbitration without privity" 10 *ICSID Review–Foreign Investment Law Journal* (1995) 232; T. Wälde, "Investment arbitration under the Energy Charter Treaty: from dispute settlement to Treaty implementation" 12 *Arbitration International* (1996) 429.

[17] Shihata and Parra, "Experience of ICSID," 344–348.

[18] ICSID Convention, Art. 26.   [19] *Ibid.*, Art. 26.

[20] See chapter 4, notes 64, 65 and associated text.   [21] ICSID Convention, Art. 54.

the individual and companies therein. An ICSID tribunal decided in the case *Fedax N.V.* v. *Venezuela* that a financial investment in promissory notes issued with the express intent of international circulation qualified as an investment under the pertinent bilateral treaty and the Convention. The tribunal regarded this as an expression of the global operation of financial markets.[22] This global nature of investments is also reflected in the fact that proceedings under ICSID may be initiated not only by private investors against states but also by states against private investors. Moreover, the claims have been brought not only by investors from developed countries against developing states, but on occasion also by those from developing countries against industrialized states.

The globalization and harmonization of dispute settlement arrangements will be further enhanced by the application of the most favored nation clause to the dispute settlement provisions of investment treaties. This approach has been confirmed by the decision of an ICSID tribunal, which has clarified the discussion which originated in the *Ambatielos*[23] and other leading international cases.[24]

The network of arrangements containing consent to ICSID, as well as the jurisprudence of ICSID, are important contributions to the harmonization of the treatment of foreign investments on a global basis, and have encouraged the flow of investments in a more certain and predictable legal environment.

Investment dispute settlement under multilateral agreements: perfecting the participation of individuals

More recently a number of multilateral agreements have strengthened the mechanisms for dispute settlement available to investors. These agreements generally follow the lines of the network of bilateral treaties discussed above, but also are innovative in some important respects.

It must be noted that guidelines on the treatment of foreign investments established under major international organizations and arrangements have regularly called for the submission of disputes to arbitration.

---

[22] ICSID, *Fedax. N.V.* v. *Republic of Venezuela*, 11 July 1997, (1998) 37 *International Legal Materials* 1378. See also in this respect chapter 3, note 51 and associated text.

[23] Award of the Commission of Arbitration established for the Ambatielos claim between Greece and the United Kingdom, dated 6 March 1956, United Nations (1963) XII *Reports of International Arbitral Awards* 91.

[24] *Emilio Agustin Maffezini* v. *Kingdom of Spain*, ICSID Case No. ARB/97/7, Decision on Jurisdiction, 25 January 2000, at www.worldbank.org/icsid/cases/awards.htm

This was the case with the 1992 World Bank Guidelines on the Treatment of Foreign Direct Investment,[25] with particular reference to ICSID, and the 1994 APEC Non-Binding Investment Principles.[26] Insofar as investments are concerned, all recent multilateral treaties have provided for arbitration accessible directly to foreign investors, sometimes including specific rules on the conduct of proceedings.

Treaties of this kind include the 1987 ASEAN Agreement for the Promotion and Protection of Investments,[27] the 1994 MERCOSUR Protocols on the Reciprocal Promotion and Protection of Investments in MERCOSUR and of investments made by countries that do not belong to this group,[28] the 1994 Free Trade Agreement between Colombia, Mexico and Venezuela,[29] and the 1994 Energy Charter Treaty.[30] In most of these treaties, as in a number of free trade agreements, dispute settlement in respect of investments is a part of parallel arrangements relating to trade and competition, thus encompassing a broad range of economic relations.

An elaborate dispute settlement arrangement is found in Chapter 11 of the North American Free Trade Agreement (NAFTA),[31] under which the investor may opt for arbitration under UNCITRAL, ICSID or its Additional Facility.[32] The definition of an investor for this purpose is broad, as it includes nationals of a state party and enterprises constituted or organized under the laws of a state party. The term "enterprise" includes partnerships, joint ventures or other forms of association,[33] as well as government-owned enterprises and states parties themselves. An entity owned or controlled by investors of a non-state party is not precluded from initiating arbitration, except that the party against which the complaint is brought may refuse to

---

[25] World Bank Guidelines on the Treatment of Foreign Direct Investment, 7 *ICSID Review– Foreign Investment Law Journal* (1992) 295.

[26] APEC Non-Binding Investment Principles, 12 November 1994, as discussed by Parra, "Provisions on settlement," 293, note 16.

[27] ASEAN Agreement for the Promotion and Protection of Investments, 15 December 1987, (1988) 27 *International Legal Materials* 612.

[28] Protocol on the Reciprocal Promotion and Protection of Investments, 17 January 1994; Protocol for the Promotion and Protection of Investments made by Countries that Do Not Belong to MERCOSUR, 5 August 1994, as discussed by Parra, "Provisions on settlement," 292, note 11.

[29] Free Trade Agreement between Colombia, Mexico and Venezuela, 13 June 1994, as discussed by Parra, "Provisions on settlement," 292, note 12.

[30] Energy Charter Treaty, 17 December 1994, 10 *ICSID Review–Foreign Investment Law Journal* (1995) 258.

[31] North American Free Trade Agreement, 17 December 1992, (1993) 32 *International Legal Materials* 605.

[32] NAFTA, Art. 1120.   [33] *Ibid.*, Art. 201.

participate if such entity has no substantial business activities in the territory of the party where it is constituted or organized.[34]

Investments are also broadly defined under NAFTA[35] where claims may be brought not only for injuries suffered by the investor directly, but also in some cases for state actions affecting its interests in an enterprise.[36] In this latter case consent of the enterprise must also be obtained,[37] although it has been argued that this requirement is not always applicable.[38] NAFTA's Chapter 14 also provides for dispute settlement arrangements in the financial services sector; some aspects relating to investments in this sector may also be submitted to the procedures available under Chapter 11.[39] Other NAFTA parties are entitled to participate in the arbitral proceedings when questions arise about the interpretation of NAFTA, which is subject to requirements of notification.[40] Claims are subject to a limitation period of three years. Questions relating to public participation and confidentiality in NAFTA will be addressed further below in conjunction with the experience of the World Trade Organization.

An interesting system of referral to the Free Trade Commission has been established in order to ensure uniformity in the interpretation of the Treaty by arbitration tribunals. An interpretation by the Commission of a provision of the Treaty is binding on the tribunal. A tribunal must request a ruling of the Commission when a party invokes the reservations or exceptions allowed under NAFTA for excluding measures from arbitration. The purpose of the request is to determine whether the measures complained of fall under such reservations or exceptions. The Commission's ruling is binding on the tribunal, but if it is not delivered within sixty days the tribunal may settle the matter itself.[41]

A number of provisions in multilateral agreements have helped to perfect the individual's participation in the proceedings and to that extent they constitute precedents that have had an influence on the general development of international dispute settlement. An important effort directed to increase the uniformity of the law applicable to foreign investments was carried out

---

[34] *Ibid.*, Art. 1113.   [35] *Ibid.*, Art. 1139.
[36] *Ibid.*, Art. 1117.   [37] *Ibid.*, Art. 1121. 2.
[38] J. Anthony Vanduzer, "Investor-state dispute settlement under NAFTA Chapter 11: the shape of things to come?" 35 *Canadian Yearbook of International Law* (1997) 263–290, at 277, note 52.
[39] *Ibid.*, 273–274.   [40] NAFTA, Arts. 1127, 1128.
[41] *Ibid.*, Art. 1132. See also generally Henri C. Alvarez, "Arbitration under the North American Free Trade Agreement", 16 *Arbitration International* (2000) 393–430; and Instituto de Investigaciones Jurídicas, Universidad Nacional Autonoma de México, *Resolución de Controversias Comerciales en América del Norte*, (1997).

under the auspices of OECD in the negotiation of a Multilateral Agreement on Investments.[42] This effort, however, failed because of policy differences arising from, among others, the fact that key developing countries were not included in the negotiations. In terms of dispute settlement the draft treaty provided for the same options as in NAFTA with the interesting addition of arbitration under the International Chamber of Commerce.[43]

Claims by individuals and the supervision of domestic determinations in international trade dispute settlement

Just like investments, trade liberalization is a powerful engine in the process of economic globalization. But unlike investors, the right of individuals and corporations engaged in international trade to access international dispute settlement has not been generally recognized. Only in some advanced agreements of economic integration and in some free trade arrangements have individuals been awarded this right, and sometimes only in a qualified manner. However, underlying trends are a clear indication that it is only a matter of time before this approach is fully recognized. While the World Trade Organization (WTO) and its elaborate dispute settlement mechanisms will be discussed later, other aspects of the trade liberalization process and dispute settlement thereunder will be discussed in the present chapter.

It must be first noted that under arrangements directed at ensuring competition in international trade, individuals are occasionally granted a right of action. This sometimes takes the form of domestic action concerning international trade, for example under the United States Trade Act of 1974 and the Omnibus Trade and Competitiveness Act of 1988, which allows interested persons to bring claims against imports or other situations involving unfair trade practices.[44] The definition of interested persons includes producers, importers, exporters, trade associations, unions or any persons representing a significant economic interest affected by the action questioned.

Sometimes the above approach is followed in a regional context, thus providing a framework for international claims of this kind, as is most notably

[42] Vanduzer, "Investor-state dispute settlement," 267.
[43] *Ibid.*, 267, note 17. See also generally the Draft Multilateral Agreement on Investments in OECD document, DAFFE/MAI/NM (98)2/REV1, 27 April 1998.
[44] 19 U.S.C. sections 2411 *et seq*. See also generally Bernd-Roland Killmann, "The access of individuals to international trade dispute settlement" 13 *Journal of International Arbitration* (1996) 143–169, at 149.

the case of the European Union. The European Union allows complaints by a Community industry, which includes producers and consumers, or more broadly by natural or legal persons, against imports affected by illicit trade practices and obstacles to trade that have an effect on the Community. This was first allowed under Regulation 2641/84 and then under Regulation 3286/94.[45] The Regulation provides for procedures and time limits for the decision of the Commission on the complaint. This does not exclude action by the individual before the European Court of Justice.[46]

A favorable decision by the Commission may lead to taking action before the WTO. Although the participation of individuals in WTO proceedings is formally excluded, having been at the origin of the complaint, the individual's links with the Commission will undoubtedly be kept active.[47] The same holds true for many state actions before the WTO dispute settlement system. Member States of the European Community may also initiate action under these regulations, an alternative which is sometimes preferred by individuals as it is less burdensome and carries a greater weight.[48] Amendments of the Regulation have been considered in order to perfect the participation by the individual in his own right.[49]

In this respect, NAFTA is an advanced model. To a large extent it follows the precedent of the Canada-United States Free Trade Agreement of 1988.[50] Although the general mechanism for dispute resolution provided for in NAFTA's Chapter 20 is only open to states parties, it does not lack innovations of general interest. Among these is the recourse to alternative dispute resolution methods, such as good offices, conciliation, mediation and expert advice.[51] Other features of interest include the intervention of scientific advice by means of the report of scientific review boards in areas such as environment and health, and the role of a highly institutionalized structure centered on the Free Trade Commission and the Secretariat.[52] An important link with the WTO is provided by the choice available to the complaining state to take the dispute either to a NAFTA panel or to the WTO.[53]

---

[45] *Official Journal*, L349/71, 31 December 1994. See discussion by Killmann, "Access of individuals," 152.
[46] *Ibid.*,156–157.   [47] *Ibid.*, 159.   [48] *Ibid.*, 159.   [49] *Ibid.*, 160–161.
[50] Canada-United States Free Trade Agreement, 22 December 1987, 2 January 1988, (1988) 27 *International Legal Materials* 281.
[51] NAFTA, Art. 2007.5.b.
[52] Harry B. Endsley, "Dispute settlement under the CFTA and NAFTA: from eleventh-hour innovation to accepted institution", 18 *Hastings International and Comparative Law Review* (1995) 659–711, at 678–680.
[53] NAFTA, Art. 2005.1.

NAFTA's Chapter 19 has established a separate dispute settlement arrangement concerning the difficult issues of anti-dumping and countervailing duties. A bi-national panel review is available to examine a request by a party in respect of the compatibility with Chapter 19 of the amendments introduced by another party to its laws in this field, or a complaint that such an amendment overturns a prior panel decision.[54] This means international judicial supervision of the legislative enactments of the parties in this field. More importantly, a panel procedure may be requested to review a final determination made by the administrative authorities of a party in respect of investigations of dumping and subsidization, for which purpose "each Party shall replace judicial review of final antidumping and countervailing duty determinations with binational panel review."[55]

This review may be requested by an affected party on its own initiative, but the request becomes mandatory if it comes from "a person who would otherwise be entitled under the law of the importing Party to commence domestic procedures for judicial determination of that final determination."[56] An interested party to this effect may be a manufacturer, producer or wholesaler of the goods in question, a recognized union, a trade or business association, or coalitions of those entities, subject to certain requirements to ensure appropriate representation.

It should also be noted that the panel review does not substitute for the review by a national judicial authority in a discretionary manner. The panel is required to apply the standard of review that each party has indicated in Annex 1911 "and the general legal principles that a court of the importing Party otherwise would apply to a review of a determination of the competent investigating authority."[57] Thus, national legislation and legal standards are applied, not by a domestic court but by a bi-national panel. This is an innovative arrangement. NAFTA parties are under the obligation not to provide for an appeal of panel decisions before domestic courts, but an Extraordinary Challenge Procedure is available.[58] This limited form of internationalization of domestic judicial functions has been criticized on legal and constitutional grounds,[59] but it has thus far endured.

---

[54] *Ibid.*, Art. 1902.   [55] *Ibid.*, Art. 1904.1.   [56] *Ibid.*, Art. 1904.5.
[57] *Ibid.*, Art. 1904.3.   [58] *Ibid.*, Art. 1904.13.
[59] Endsley, "Dispute Settlement" 672, note 77. See also generally Eric J. Pan: "Assessing the NAFTA Chapter 19 binational panel system: an experiment in international adjudication", 40 *Harvard International Law Journal* (1999) 379–449.

The settlement of private commercial disputes is also encouraged under NAFTA by means of arbitration and alternative dispute resolution methods.[60] A court or administrative body may wish to request the view of a party to NAFTA if an issue of interpretation or application of the Agreement arises in the course of these proceedings, or a Party may wish to intervene. In such cases the Agreement provides for a process of notifications and for the Free Trade Commission to endeavor to agree on the appropriate response, but if there is no agreement any party may ultimately submit its own views to the requesting court or entity.[61] This kind of referral mechanism serves the uniform interpretation and application of the Agreement. Both the 1958 Convention on the Recognition and Enforcement of Foreign Arbitral Awards[62] and the Inter-American Convention on International Commercial Arbitration[63] are referred to in NAFTA in the context of observance of agreements to arbitrate and enforcement of arbitral awards.[64] An Advisory Committee on Private Commercial Disputes[65] and a similar Committee on Private Commercial Disputes regarding Agricultural Goods[66] have also been established for the purpose of assisting in the use and effectiveness of dispute resolution between private parties.

Private parties have also been authorized to participate in some NAFTA dispute settlement mechanisms or examination arrangements, such as the review and appeal of determinations of origin[67] or complaints under the Agreement on Environmental Cooperation.[68]

These mechanisms and procedures reveal a sustained pattern of recognition of individuals' participation in trade-related dispute settlement arrangements, which in some respects anticipates the need for similar approaches in other trade liberalization agreements. These arrangements also evidence the development of international judicial supervision of legislative activity by states parties in some fields and of determinations made by national authorities.

---

[60] NAFTA, Art. 2022.1.   [61] *Ibid.*, Art. 2020.

[62] United Nations Convention on the Recognition and Enforcement of Foreign Arbitral Awards, 10 June 1958, 330 UNTS 38.

[63] Inter-American Convention on International Commercial Arbitration, 30 January 1975, (1975) 14 *International Legal Materials* 336.

[64] NAFTA, Art. 2022.2, 3.   [65] *Ibid.*, Art. 2022.4.

[66] *Ibid.*, Art. 707.   [67] *Ibid.*, Art. 510.

[68] North American Agreement on Environmental Cooperation, and discussion by Leon E. Trakman, *Dispute Settlement under the NAFTA* (1997), pp. 31–35.

Dispute settlement in advanced economic integration: federalization of institutions and efficient operation of markets

To the extent that economic relations reach advanced levels of integration, particularly in terms of customs unions and common market schemes, the dispute settlement procedures move to a greater degree of participation by individuals. In some cases, for example in the European Union, this is the result of the transfer by states of some of their powers to common institutions, while in other situations it simply relates to the need to ensure an efficient operation of markets.

The paramount example of an advanced dispute settlement system in the context of economic integration is that of the European Community Court of Justice (ECJ), with the Court of First Instance instituted in 1989.[69] The general jurisdiction of the ECJ in infringement actions against Member States, judicial review of the legality of acts of Community organs and rulings on the interpretation of the Treaty and other acts, reveals that it is not just a dispute settlement body. In fact, it comes closer to a high federal court that may exercise in some respects constitutional functions. The right of the ECJ to review decisions of the Court of First Instance also confirms this higher function.

The jurisdiction of the ECJ in respect of actions brought by individuals is particularly significant.[70] This applies first to actions relating to the annulment of decisions affecting a natural or juridical person directly and individually. The capacity of individuals to bring action follows their capacity

---

[69] Decision No. 88/591, 24 October 1988, *Official Journal* L319, 25 November 1988. On the Court of First Instance see generally R. Joliet and W. Vogell, "Le tribunal de premiere instance des communautés européennes" 329 *Revue du Marché Commun* (1989) 424; and Rafael García-Valdecasas y Fernández, "El tribunal de primera instancia de las comunidades Eeuropeas" in Gil Carlos Rodriguez Iglesias and Diego J. Liñan Nogueras (eds.), *El Derecho Comunitario Europeo y su Aplicación Judicial* (1995), p. 403. For a discussion of initiatives concerning the establishment of regional courts, specialized courts and a constitutional court supplementing the system under the ECJ, see José Luis Da Cruz Vilaça, "La protection des droits des particuliers et le systéme juridictionnel communautaire dans le Traité d'Amsterdam" in Juan Manuel de Faramiñán Gilbert (Coordinador), *Reflexiones en Torno al Tratado de Amsterdam y el Futuro de la Unión Europea* (2000), pp. 245–271. See also Liz Hefferman, "The Community courts post-Nice: a European *certiorari* revisited" 52 *ICLQ* (2003) 907–933.

[70] Henry Schermers and Denis Waelbroeck, *Judicial Protection in the European Communities* (1987); José Carlos Moitinho de Almeida, "Evolución jurisprudencial en materia de acceso de los particulares a la jurisdicción comunitaria" in Rodriguez and Liñan *El Derecho*, p. 595. See also Da Cruz Vilaça, "La Protection des droits," 245–271.

under national legislation, irrespective of nationality requirements;[71] legal entities include those created under private or public law, and even actions by entities devoid of legal personality have been occasionally admitted.[72] The test of individual interest has been applied, however, in a restrictive manner.[73] Actions by individuals against omission by institutions that have failed to act, in violation of the Treaty, basically follow the same pattern.[74]

A separate heading of jurisdiction relates to claims for compensation of damages arising from liability of the community institutions.[75] Disputes relating to contracts, however, are normally submitted to national jurisdictions, except when the ECJ is entitled to pass judgment under a special clause in contracts done by the Community or on its behalf, or in other specific circumstances.[76] The ECJ also has jurisdiction in administrative disputes concerning the officials of the Community.[77]

The functions of the ECJ in interpreting Community law in the context of the referral mechanism by national courts is also a particularly relevant aspect of its jurisdiction,[78] and significantly contributes to the uniformity and consistency of such interpretation. There has been some thought of adapting this mechanism in cases of association of the Community with other institutions or countries in order to ensure that the context of the case or a legal tradition be duly taken into consideration.[79] The referral mechanism has also been considered with respect to other dispute settlement arrangements and, as discussed above, could well serve as a model for the International Court of Justice and other international tribunals.[80]

While in the more general scheme of a free trade area embodied in the Latin American Integration Association established in 1980, dispute settlement was basically concerned with inter-state procedures relating to the interpretation, application and observance of the treaty rules, occasionally

---

[71] M. Waelbroeck, J.V. Louis and G. Vandersanden, "Le droit de la Communauté Economique Européenne" in *La Cour de Justice, les Actes des Institutions* (1983), vol. 10, 103.

[72] Moitinho de Almeida, "Evolución jurisprudencial," 596–597.

[73] *Ibid.*, 619.   [74] *Ibid.*, 620–622.   [75] *Ibid.*, 623.   [76] *Ibid.*, 630.

[77] European Community Treaty, Art. 179.   [78] Ibid., Art. 177 (new Art. 234).

[79] During the negotiations for an European Economic Area a joint integration of the European Court of Justice and the EFTA states was considered in the context of dispute settlement, for which see Christophe Reymond, "Institutions, decision-making procedure and settlement of disputes in the European Economic Area" 30 *Common Market Law Review* (1993) 449–480, at 455–456. Also a Greek *ad hoc* judge at the ECJ was discussed for the settlement of disputes in the Agreement of Association.

[80] See chapter 2, notes 69, 70 and associated text.

the access by individuals was considered in various proposals.[81] Some proposals provided for such participation, subject to the requirement of residence in a member country or carrying on business there. Claims for damage would be allowed if they arose from measures adopted by states or common institutions in violation of treaty commitments, but in any event such action would have to be taken before national bodies designated by each country. Although these proposals were not implemented, trade liberalization agreements made between two or more countries of the Association developed the dispute settlement arrangements to a greater extent and included those relating to the protection of investments.[82]

Because the Common Market of the Southern Cone (MERCOSUR) involves the establishment of a customs union, the limited provisions for inter-state dispute settlement contained in the Treaty establishing the union in 1991 had soon to be supplemented by special protocols.[83] These arrangements provide for arbitration in inter-state disputes concerning the interpretation, application and observance of agreed rules and of the decisions adopted by the common institutions.[84] More importantly, individuals are also entitled to bring action for damages against measures adopted by states or the common institutions that might be restrictive of trade, discriminatory or distort competition.[85]

These actions are brought before national sections of the common market where the individual has residence or a corporation conducts business, independently from their nationality. The national section will either seek a solution with the national section of the country whose measures are subject to the complaint or directly place the claim before the common market group or the Trade Commission, where the individual and the defendant state have the right to state their case.[86] Expert groups may be established and ultimately arbitration might follow. In spite of the more

---

[81] Ernesto J. Rey Caro, *La Solución de Controversias en Los Procesos de Integración en América. El MERCOSUR* (1998), pp. 22–24. See also generally Antonio Martínez Puñal, *La Solución de Controversias en el Mercado Común del Sur (MERCOSUR): Estudio de sus Mecanismos* (2000).

[82] *Ibid.*, p. 24. See further Angela Del Vecchio (ed.), *Aspetti dell' Integrazione Regionale Latinoamericana* (2001). See also note 29 in respect of the Free Trade Agreement between Colombia, Mexico and Venezuela.

[83] See MERCOSUR Protocol for the Settlement of Disputes, 17 December 1991, and its amendments, in Rey Caro, *La Solución*, pp. 97, 109, 111. See also the MERCOSUR Protocol on the Settlement of Disputes (Protocol of Olivos), 18 February 2002, and Ernesto J. Rey Caro, *El Protocolo de Olivos para la Solucion de Controversias en el MERCOSUR* (2002).

[84] See for example the award of the arbitral tribunal in a trade dispute between Argentina and Brazil, 28 April 1999.

[85] Rey Caro, *La Solución*, pp. 58–59.   [86] *Ibid.*, p. 61.

elaborate structure of these arrangements, they are still insufficient to deal with the needs and difficulties faced by an advanced common market and it is expected that they might evolve accordingly.

Following the tradition of the early Central American Court of Justice,[87] the process of integration of the countries of this area has led to the establishment in 1992 of a new Court of Justice.[88] The new court has jurisdiction over disputes submitted by any state party, except in some matters, such as boundary disputes, where all the parties to the dispute have to consent to the jurisdiction of the court. It also has jurisdiction over disputes between private parties or between private parties and the common institutions, particularly in respect of the annulment of decisions affecting such individuals and the observance of treaty and other rules. Individuals may bring action before the court in a number of matters, including non-compliance with judicial decisions.[89] It also serves as an administrative tribunal for the staff of the common institutions.

Supreme Courts of each state party may refer to the court questions of treaty interpretation, while other domestic courts may refer to it questions of interpretation of the basic rules of the process of integration. The court has also been equipped with advisory jurisdiction. It is particularly interesting that the court may intervene as a constitutional court in respect of disputes or disagreements between main organs of the state at the request of the affected body, particularly in cases of non-compliance with judicial decisions.

The Andean Community has established a Court of Justice as well, which follows very closely the model of the European Community. Actions on infringement, annulment, omission and interpretation may be brought before the court also by individuals.[90] However, because the nature of this integration scheme is so different from the European model, the Court of Justice has a limited role.

Various arrangements for dispute settlement associated with schemes of advanced economic integration demonstrate that their particular characteristics are mainly the result of specific operational needs for the most efficient functioning of the market, with particular reference to free trade, competition and investments. It is in this light that the role of the individual

---

[87] See chapter 4, note 4 and associated text.

[88] Statute of the Central American Court of Justice, 10 December 1992, in *Corte Centroamericana de Justicia*, (1998), p. 408.

[89] See, e.g., Case No. 30.9, on action against the Judiciary of Nicaragua for failure to comply with a decision, 5 December 1996, in *Ibid.*, p. 119.

[90] Treaty establishing the Andean Court of Justice, 1979, and Protocol of Amendments of 28 May 1996, and comments by Rey Caro, *La Solución*, pp. 26–32. See also the Treaty establishing the Caribbean Court of Justice, 14 February 2001.

has been, or is being recognized, as an essential feature of such operation. Such characteristics are also the result of the traditions and understandings of the states concerned. It is for this reason that models developed in one regional context are not always useful or appropriate for another region, particularly when they respond to a quasi-federal institutional structure.

Private entities and dispute resolution in international organizations

Another noteworthy development concerns dispute settlement mechanisms and associated procedures devised in the context of international organizations and directed at specific needs of individuals and private entities.

The establishment of administrative tribunals within major international organizations is an important precedent in respect of direct access of certain categories of individuals to international tribunals,[91] an approach that could well be followed in other types of arrangements involving individual rights and interests. The twentieth anniversary of the establishment of the World Bank Administrative Tribunal, one of the leading institutions in the field, has highlighted the practice of a number of these tribunals. For this purpose, a broad survey was undertaken, which included the tribunals of the Asian Development Bank, the International Monetary Fund, the African Development Bank, the Organization for Economic Cooperation and Development, the Council of Europe, the North Atlantic Treaty Organization, the Organization of American States, the European Space Agency, the Inter-American Development Bank, the United Nations and the International Labor Organization.[92]

The practice of these tribunals demonstrates that their work is not exclusively related to administrative matters, but also covers the review of legislation to the extent related to the rights of staff members.[93] In the leading case of *de Merode*, the World Bank Administrative Tribunal made a first step in

---

[91] C.F. Amerasinghe, *The Law of the International Civil Service* (1994).

[92] Nassib G. Ziadé, "Some practical issues arising in International Administrative Tribunals," Paper presented at Conference on the Commemoration of the Twentieth Anniversary of the World Bank Administrative Tribunal, Paris, 16 May 2000.

[93] Michel Gentot, "Review of discretionary power by international administrative tribunals"; Nicolas Valticos: "Checks exerted by administrative tribunals over the discretionary powers of international organizations"; Francisco Orrego Vicuña: "The review of managerial discretion by international administrative tribunals: comments in the light of the practice of the World Bank Administrative Tribunal," papers presented to the conference on the Commemoration of the Twentieth Anniversary of the World Bank Administrative Tribunal, Paris, 16 May 2000.

the review of administrative policies that might affect fundamental elements of the rights and duties of staff members.[94] It then introduced a meaningful limitation in the exercise of discretion in this context, holding that such elements, unlike those that are less fundamental, cannot be changed without the consent of the staff member concerned. A second step relates to the regular review by tribunals of legislation that entails discrimination or other anomalies.

Recently, however, the need has arisen to take this review a step further. This occurred in connection with new World Bank rules on pension reform. In *Crevier* and subsequent cases, the applicant and the Staff Association raised, in addition to claims of discrimination and related questions, an objection to the very objective pursued by the reform and its philosophy, independently from the manner of how it could affect an individual staff member.[95] The tribunal examined every single aspect of the contentions in order to establish the reasonableness and fairness of the Bank's legislation, which was ultimately upheld. It follows that legislation can also be reviewed, subject to certain limitations.

The function of review is exercised regularly by tribunals and other bodies without the threat of establishing the supremacy of an organ over another, which would be wholly unwarranted in the case of international organizations and their administrative tribunals. The sole objective of this function is to ensure fully the safeguard of the rights of individual staff members under the rule of law and the prevention of arbitrariness.

A different development is the creation of the World Bank Inspection Panel. This arrangement allows for the review of operations, not in the capacity of a commission of inquiry or implied mediation or adjudication, but as a mechanism that enhances quality control in the design and implementation of projects, ensuring a greater institutional transparency and accountability.[96]

---

[94] World Bank Administrative Tribunal, *de Merode*, Decision No. 1, 1981, paras. 41, 42.

[95] World Bank Administrative Tribunal, *Crevier*, Decision No. 205, 1999.

[96] Ibrahim F. I. Shihata, "The World Bank Inspection Panel: its historical, legal and operational aspects" in Shihata, *The World Bank in a Changing World* (2000), pp. 537–601 (hereinafter cited as *Changing World*). See also Laurence Boisson de Chazournes, "Public participation in decision-making: the World Bank Inspection Panel" in Edith Brown Weiss, Andres Rigo Sureda and Laurence Boisson de Chazournes (eds.), *The World Bank, International Financial Institutions, and the Development of International Law*, American Society of International Law Studies in Transnational Legal Policy No. 31 (1999), pp. 84–94; Sabine Schlemmer-Schulte, "Introductory note to the conclusions of the second review of the World Bank Inspection Panel," (2000) 39 *International Legal Materials* 243; Ibrahim F.I. Shihata, *The World Bank Inspection Panel* (2000).

A most significant feature of this mechanism is the capacity to bring complaints directly before an international forum by private parties affected by a given project, such as organizations, associations or other groupings of individuals.[97] Individuals must show that their rights and interests have been adversely and directly affected by an action or omission of the Bank. The Inspection Panel has been conceived as part of a broader policy of public participation in the Bank's policies and project development. The following contributions resulting from this mechanism have been noted:

It is an institutional bridge between partners of different legal standing, whereby individuals are provided with a means of redress in an international forum for actions attributable to an international organization. Indeed, one of the most interesting features of the Inspection Panel is that participation by non-state actors is formalized and that the procedure has been agreed upon by the member states of the organization. It is also an innovative dispute resolution strategy that contributes towards the broadening of the accountability of an international organization.[98]

This procedure has been rightly described as "a progressive step in the development of both the law of international organizations and the international law of human rights."[99]

The practice of international organizations has been increasingly receptive to taking into account the need for public participation in decision-making. Following the tradition of participation of non-governmental organizations in the work of the United Nations Economic and Social Council and related bodies by means of the recognition of a consultative status, this kind of arrangement has extended to some other organizations. This is particularly the case of the United Nations Conference on Trade and Development, the OECD, the International Monetary Fund and the World Bank, where a special committee to this effect has been set up.[100] Other arrangements for participation are provided under the United Nations Conference for Environment and Development, the Convention on Biological Diversity and the North American Agreement for Environmental Cooperation.[101]

Participation in dispute settlement procedures is also available in several instances, particularly before the European Court of Human Rights, the

---

[97] Richard E. Bissell, "Recent practice of the Inspection Panel of the World Bank" 91 *American Journal of International Law* (1997) 741–744.
[98] Boisson de Chazournes, "Public Participation," 94.
[99] Shihata, *Changing World*, p. 601.
[100] International Centre for Trade and Sustainable Development, *Accreditation Schemes and Other Arrangements for Public Participation in International Fora* (November 1999), p. 11.
[101] *Ibid.*, pp. 10–13.

Inter-American Commission of Human Rights and the Inter-American Court of Human Rights. In the latter case, independent representation and the submission of *amicus curiae* briefs are allowed as a matter of routine.[102]

As has been noted above, however, the possibility of increased participation by non-governmental organizations in dispute settlement arrangements and generally in international organizations will largely depend on the professionalism that such entities might demonstrate, an element which presently is still far from evident in many cases.[103]

Corporate and other entities before the International Tribunal for the Law of the Sea

Because of the active involvement of corporate entities in the undertaking of seabed mining, the Law of the Sea Convention had to facilitate their participation in the arrangements under Part XI. Two steps were taken to this effect. The first, a rather modest one, was to allow the sponsorship of an entity applying for a contract, not only by the state of nationality but also by the state exercising the effective control of such entity, thus following the trends on corporate control already evident in international law.[104]

The second step, a more significant one, was to provide for the compulsory jurisdiction of the Seabed Disputes Chamber to apply also to private contractors, both in respect of disputes between parties to contracts and between the Seabed Authority and prospective contractors.[105] Contractual, pre-contractual and tortious liability are thereby brought under the jurisdiction of the Chamber. Issues such as the interpretation and application of contracts, refusal of a contract, legal issues arising in the negotiation of a contract and acts or omissions directed to the other party or directly affecting its legitimate interests may fall under this jurisdiction.[106] Disputes

---

[102] *Ibid.*, p. 16.   [103] See chapter 2, note 66 and associated text.

[104] American Law Institute, Restatement of the Law Third, *The Foreign Relations Law of the United States* (1987), vol. 1, p. 268.

[105] United Nations Convention on the Law of the Sea, Arts. 186–191, and discussion by Allan E. Boyle, "Settlement of disputes relating to the law of the sea and the environment" in *Thesaurus Acroasium*, vol. XXVI, International Justice (1997), pp. 299–356, at 307, 335–336, 340–341. See also generally Thomas A. Mensah, "The role of peaceful dispute settlement in contemporary ocean policy" in Davor Vidas and Willy Ostreng, *Order for the Oceans at the Turn of the Century* (1999), pp. 81–94, and Thomas A. Mensah, "The dispute settlement regime of the 1982 United Nations Convention on the Law of the Sea" 2 *Max Planck Yearbook of United Nations Law* (1998), 307–323.

[106] Boyle, "Settlement of disputes," 340, with particular reference to Law of the Sea Convention Art. 187.

concerning the interpretation and application of a contract may also be submitted to binding commercial arbitration, except that issues relating to the interpretation of the Convention must be referred to the tribunal Chamber.[107]

It is also of interest to note that the Seabed Authority may bring action against states for violations of Part XI and related annexes, just as states may bring action against the Seabed Authority for similar violations or for excess of jurisdiction or misuse of power.[108] It has been rightly noted that to this extent the Chamber will be exercising a power of judicial review, but within strict limits established in the Convention.[109]

In other matters, such as the prompt release of vessels and crews, an application before the tribunal must be made by or on behalf of the flag state.[110] This is so although in these situations the interest of private parties and crews will be most relevant. However, it is felt that the sponsorship of the flag state is necessary to keep a minimum of control. Such sponsorship might turn out to be more nominal than real, particularly in respect of flags of convenience.

The International Tribunal for the Law of the Sea also has jurisdiction over cases submitted under agreements conferring such jurisdiction with the acceptance of all the parties to a particular dispute.[111] It has been suggested that this provision is not necessarily restricted to cases in which the parties are states.[112] According to this interpretation, the parties could "equally well be NGOs or international organisations, corporations, or private individuals."[113] It has also been argued that in any event private parties, international organizations and states could bring cases to the tribunal by special agreement, and that the possibility of bringing public interest actions is left unresolved, but not necessarily excluded.[114] Even if some aspects of the above interpretation may be open to question, overall it does respond to a trend that is developing throughout the international dispute settlement system. At some point the question might have to be addressed.

---

[107] Boyle, "Settlement of disputes," 341, with particular reference to Law of the Sea Convention Art. 188(2).
[108] Law of the Sea Convention Art. 187(a), (b).
[109] Boyle, "Settlement of disputes," 338–339.
[110] Law of the Sea Convention Art. 292.
[111] Law of the Sea Convention Annex VI, Art. 20.
[112] Boyle, "Settlement of disputes," 332–333.
[113] *Ibid.*, 332. The Rules of the Tribunal provide for various requests of information from inter-governmental organizations, in particular in Arts. 57.2 and 84.
[114] Boyle, "Settlement of disputes," 332–333.

Establishing an International Environmental Court

Many of the developments that have been outlined in this chapter have led to the proposal to establish an International Environmental Court.[115] This initiative is not only based on environmental considerations. Among other considerations there is the need for a specialized jurisdiction in this field, access by individuals and groups to international procedures, the participation of international organizations as parties to disputes and the overall need to represent, through such a court, the common interest of the international community.

It is evident that environmental issues are significant for the international community. This will probably lead to a greater awareness of the need to find adequate solutions in this field, including dispute settlement. However, it is not certain that an International Environmental Court will be the necessary outcome of this process. It has been rightly explained that environmental expertise cannot be isolated from expertise in international law and other relevant areas. It is also noted that existing courts and tribunals have successfully handled several disputes of this kind.[116]

Access by individuals and groups to international procedures is developing on its own merits, not just in relation to environmental matters, and this trend is likely to continue. The World Bank Inspection Panel and other similar institutions provide an example of how this need may be addressed and involve recognition of the accountability of international organizations before the international community. It is also to be expected that international organizations might participate as parties to international dispute settlement procedures, as has already been recognized, albeit indirectly. Even the right of action of one international organization against another one should not be excluded in this evolving scenario.

Questions relating to the representation of community interests are also part of a more general agenda in international dispute settlement. These include the issue of an *actio popularis* discussed above, which is not yet quite ripe for implementation.[117] In the meantime, national law and national courts, interacting with international law and its institutions, are likely to contribute significantly.[118]

Environmental issues are likely to be part of more complex disputes involving questions of trade, production, investment, rights of the individual,

---

[115] Alfred Rest, "The indispensability of an International Environmental Court" 7 *Review of European Community and International Environmental Law* (1998) 63–67 and discussion of these initiatives by Ellen Hey, *Reflections on an International Environmental Court* (2000).

[116] *Ibid.*, pp. 2, 7–9.   [117] *Ibid.*, pp. 21–24.   [118] *Ibid.*, p. 20.

policy of international organizations and other matters that are inseparable from the general body of international law and its governing institutions.

Changing scenario of international dispute settlement

The developments and practice that have been examined show that the settlement of international disputes has significantly changed in the past few decades and is still rapidly changing in virtually every contemporary arrangement. It may be argued that many of these arrangements are peculiar to very specific situations or respond to the needs of particular circumstances that do not necessarily transcend into the broader outlook for dispute settlement in the international community. It has been also argued, as noted above, that the innovative legal solutions embodied in these developments are *lex specialis* and do not alter the standing principles of international law.

Notwithstanding such arguments, when the aggregate of the practice is examined, covering a significant period of time, and many regions and institutions, there can be little doubt that the scenario for dispute settlement has indeed changed and that its innovations have become an inspiration for an increasing number of similar arrangements.

Another criterion needs to be taken into consideration. It was mentioned at the beginning of this chapter that a number of these developments respond to the needs of globalization and the introduction of market economies across the world, including the operation of international markets. This is particularly so in the case of investments, trade and other forms of economic cooperation. These activities represent the highest proportion of international affairs in the contemporary world and hence also disputes concerning these matters are the most common. If most of these disputes are submitted to new institutions and procedures, the traditional inter-state dispute settlement mechanisms will be used less frequently and perhaps even in an exceptional manner. The exception then becomes the rule and the *lex specialis* becomes the *lex generalis*. While this process is certainly not complete, it is evidently underway.

6

The World Trade Organization integrated dispute settlement system: innovation and transition

The previous chapters have shown that international society is moving towards a more centralized system of public justice, with more emphasis on what can properly be described as "constitutional" issues. At the same time, a degree of decentralization may be noted: this takes the form of direct access of individuals to international courts and tribunals, and their participation in other procedures, most notably in specialized jurisdictions. At first sight, this coexsitence of centralization and decentralization may appear as a fundamental contradiction that could result in adverse prospects for dispute settlement. It is suggested that this is not the case.

Indeed, both trends are gradually developing or are likely to develop links and interrelations that could result in a more structured and integrated system of international dispute settlement. Such a development would be an important step forward: both public and private mechanisms could be combined, taking into account both states and individuals. An example is the World Trade Organization, where an integrated dispute settlement system has been put in place and where gradually the role of the individual is being recognized.

Combining dispute settlement methods in an integrated system

A salient feature of the WTO Dispute Settlement Understanding (DSU)[1] is that it has been structured as an integrated system. Not only is this so

---

[1] Understanding on Rules and Procedures Governing the Settlement of Disputes, Annex 2 to the Marrakesh Agreement Establishing the World Trade Organization, 15 April 1994 (hereinafter cited as DSU).

because it covers disputes under the many instruments that compose the legal framework of the World Trade Organization[2] but also because it provides for various methods of dispute settlement, all of the above under the central administration of the Dispute Settlement Body.[3] The system thus has a broad jurisdictional coverage and also gives the disputants some choice, albeit somewhat limited, as to the method of solving potential disputes. Under the DSU the first step in case of a dispute are consultations between the parties, with the possibility to request the establishment of a panel if no satisfactory solution is found within sixty days. There is thus a strong incentive for a negotiated settlement.[4] If a solution is reached at any time of the dispute settlement process it must be consistent with the pertinent agreements and must not nullify or impair benefits accruing to any member under those agreements.[5] A request for consultations is subject to a notification procedure[6] and there is the possibility of intervention by other parties that claim a substantial interest in the matter.[7]

The parties also have the option of submitting a dispute to political methods such as good offices, conciliation and mediation.[8] Again, if no solution is reached within set time limits the complaining party may request the establishment of a panel.[9] An interesting feature is that these procedures may continue, subject to the agreement of the parties, while the panel proceeds.[10] The Director General may offer *ex officio* good offices, conciliation and mediation,[11] and when the case involves a least-developed country that official or the Chairman of the Dispute Settlement Body will make such offer at the request of that least-developed country.[12] While in the above cases the officials will have a leading role in the conduct of these proceedings, there is nothing to prevent the parties from agreeing on an alternative

---

[2] Appendix 1 of the DSU contains the list of the Agreements covered by the Understanding, while Appendix 2 lists special or additional Rules and Procedures contained in the covered agreements.

[3] Ernst-Ulrich Petersmann, "The dispute settlement system of the World Trade Organization and the evolution of the GATT dispute settlement system since 1948" 31 *Common Market Law Review* (1994) 1157–1244, at 1207. See also generally the "Symposium on the first three years of the WTO dispute settlement system" 32 *The International Lawyer* (1998) 609 *et seq*; Ernst-Ulrich Petersmann, *The GATT/WTO Dispute Settlement System: International Law, International Organizations, and Dispute Settlement* (1996); James Cameron and Karen Campbell, *Dispute Resolution in the World Trade Organisation* (1998); David Palmeter and Petros C. Mavroidis, *Dispute Settlement in the World Trade Organization* (1999); John H. Jackson, *The Jurisprudence of GATT and the WTO* (2000); Friedl Weiss (ed.), *Improving WTO Dispute Settlement Procedures* (2000).

[4] DSU, Art. 4.7.   [5] DSU, Art. 3.5.   [6] DSU, Art. 4.4.   [7] DSU, Art. 4.11.
[8] DSU, Art. 5.   [9] DSU, Art. 5.4.   [10] DSU, Art. 5.5.   [11] DSU, Art. 5.6.
[12] DSU, Art. 24.

method to settle the dispute. According to Article 3.7 of the DSU a solution mutually acceptable to both parties to a dispute and consistent with the covered agreements is "clearly to be preferred."

Apart from political methods the DSU also provides for legal methods of solving disputes under WTO rules. The most significant of these is the mandatory panel procedure that must be followed at the request of a complaining party.[13] The panel's task is to examine the case in the light of the relevant provisions of the agreement concerned and to make the findings that will allow the Dispute Settlement Body to make recommendations or give an appropriate ruling.[14] The difficult process of establishing a panel under the GATT 1947, has now been replaced by an almost automatic right of the complaining party to submit the dispute to a panel, subject to certain conditions and timetables.

An important innovation introduced in the WTO, as compared with its predecessor the GATT 1947, is the establishment of a standing Appellate Body to which parties to a dispute may appeal the panel report.[15] The Appellate Body may uphold, modify or reverse the legal findings and conclusions of the panel.[16] To this date, the parties have usually availed themselves of the right to appeal. On the basis of panel and Appellate Body reports the Dispute Settlement Body then adopts the pertinent recommendations and rulings.

The DSU also allows for arbitration "as an alternative means of dispute settlement,"[17] an option that requires the agreement of the parties and which is also potentially open to third party intervention if the original parties so accept.[18] Expeditious arbitration is now also available provided that pursuant to Article 25 the issues are clearly defined by both parties. Other forms of arbitration are also included in the DSU.[19] The Dispute Settlement Body surveillance of implementation and possible authorization of compensation and suspension of concessions also applies in the context of arbitral decisions.[20]

Two mechanisms for the enforcement of international obligations have also been included within the WTO framework. One is the surveillance by the Dispute Settlement Body of the compliance and implementation of adopted recommendations and rulings;[21] the other is the resort to compensation or the suspension of concessions, as a kind of sanction related to

---

[13] DSU, Arts. 6–16.   [14] DSU, Art. 7.   [15] DSU, Art. 17.   [16] DSU, Art. 17.13.

[17] DSU, Art. 25.1. See also Laurence Boisson de Chazournes, "L'arbitrage à L'OMC" 3 *Revue de l'Arbitrage* (2003) 949–988.

[18] DSU, Art. 25.2, 3.   [19] DSU, Arts. 21.3 and 22.6.   [20] DSU, Art. 25.4.

[21] DSU, Art. 21.

the objective of compliance and implementation.[22] The latter mechanism is temporary in nature and subject to a number of requirements, as well as the possibility of requesting arbitration in case of a dispute as to the level of suspension of concessions.[23] It will be examined further below. This type of mechanism finds frequent application in the context of environmental arrangements and other matters where prevention plays an important role.

This extensive combination of political and legal methods, coupled with the integrated dispute settlement approach, is characteristic of GATT/WTO. In making available alternative dispute resolution options in conjunction with mandatory legal procedures, the WTO has attained an interesting balance between the need to rely on the rule of law and the necessary flexibility to accommodate situations that are often new or unprecedented. This model, occasionally referred to as a quasi-judicial model,[24] serves well the dynamic nature of international trade and transactions, and has been reinforced by the trends that will be discussed next.

Developing a judicial function with flexibility under the WTO

The experience with the dispute settlement arrangements under the GATT 1947 showed that the system had a number of shortcomings, particularly the fragmentation of procedures, difficulties and delays in the adoption of panel reports and frequent non-compliance with the decisions taken in the course of these procedures.[25] In spite of these difficulties, however, the GATT experience also showed that there was a gradual evolution from a rather diplomatic form of dispute settlement culture to one premised on the rule of law.[26] An important change that took place in this context was the "de-politicization" of the panel procedure.[27] The establishment of the WTO and the innovations introduced by the DSU made a specific and valuable contribution to this development, while at the same time keeping the essential flexibility of the system.

As rightly put by Jackson, the rule-oriented approach to dispute settlement has the important advantage of leading "to greater certainty and predictability – essential in international affairs, particularly *economic* affairs

---

[22] DSU, Art. 22.   [23] DSU, Art. 22.6.

[24] See generally M.E. Hudec, *Enforcing International Trade Law, The Evolution of the Modern GATT Legal System* (1993).

[25] Petersmann, "Dispute settlement system," 1203–1204.

[26] *Ibid.*, 1187–1189.   [27] *Ibid.*, 1188.

driven by market-oriented principles of decentralized decision-making, with participation of millions of entrepreneurs."[28] This means in practice that the dispute settlement system of international trade has gradually adjusted to the needs of a market-economy approach prevailing in the international community.

The establishment of the Appellate Body has provided for a strengthened legal framework for the consideration of disputes after their examination by a panel, thus significantly contributing to the needs of uniformity in the interpretation of WTO rules. There has also been another significant innovation. The consensus procedure required under the GATT 1947 for the adoption of panel reports, which was at the root of the difficulties and delays, has been effectively reversed. The Dispute Settlement Body will now adopt a panel report unless it is appealed by one of the parties. The decision of the Appellate Body will in turn be adopted by the Dispute Settlement Body and unconditionally accepted by the parties to the dispute unless this Body "decides by consensus not to adopt the Appellate Body report" within thirty days of the circulation of the report.[29]

The process of transformation of the dispute settlement system within the GATT/WTO has not been free of problems. At the base of such difficulties is the question of the nature of obligations under the GATT/WTO. The view has been held that following the GATT traditions, there is still much room for diplomatic maneuvering and that in this light the nature of legal obligations under the WTO is merely recommendatory, the system resting on voluntary compliance.[30] The contrary view, however, is that there is enough evidence to support the conclusion that obligations for the parties to the WTO are legally binding in the full sense.[31]

Connected with the above question is that concerning the legal nature of the panel reports. Under GATT Article XXIII, the contracting parties may, in respect of the matters referred to them, "make appropriate recommendations to the Contracting Parties which they consider to be concerned, or

[28] John H. Jackson, *The World Trade Organization. Constitution and Jurisprudence* (1998), pp. 60–61.

[29] DSU, Art. 17.14. See also Jackson, *The WTO*, p. 72.

[30] Judith Hippler Bello, "The WTO Dispute Settlement Understanding: less is more" 90 *American Journal of International Law* (1996) 416, at 416–417. See also generally Hannes L. Schloemann and Stefan Ohlhoff, "'Constitutionalization' and dispute settlement in the WTO: national security as an issue of competence" 93 *American Journal of International Law* (1999) 424–451.

[31] Jackson, *The WTO*, pp. 85–89. See also John H. Jackson, "The WTO Dispute Settlement Understanding: misunderstandings on the nature of legal obligations" 91 *American Journal of International Law* (1997) 60.

give a ruling on the matter, as appropriate."[32] The language of the DSU did not address the question whether such reports are binding on the parties to the dispute, nor whether there was an option to compensate for any inconsistency in conduct found by a panel to exist.[33]

The view that reports are binding is persuasive, in part because the language of the DSU strongly emphasizes the need for compliance with recommendations and rulings in order "to ensure effective resolution of disputes to the benefit of all Members."[34] While the issue of compliance with rulings and recommendations is of course different from that of the legal nature of panel reports, strengthening the legal obligation to comply will in turn result in a more effective dispute settlement system. This is also an area where developments might be expected in the near future.

Furthermore, the innovations noted above of introducing supervisory functions and the resort to temporary sanctions, such as compensation or the suspension of concessions, which are conceived to encourage the implementation of panel reports, are also a part of a broader process of ensuring compliance with recommendations and rulings.

The conclusion suggested above is also persuasive in part because a binding report or decision is the only possible outcome of legal procedures such as an appeal before the Appellate Body or arbitration as an alternative dispute resolution method. It would be rather unusual to have a decision by an appeals body or an arbitral award that is not supported by its essential binding legal nature. It is also important to note that practice, as confirmed by the Appellate Body, supports the binding legal nature of adopted reports.[35]

A distinguished member of the Appellate Body has concluded that the legal obligation of members to bring all their disputes relating to the application and implementation of the covered agreements to the WTO dispute settlement system amounts to the establishment of "compulsory jurisdiction."[36] In this context it is also noted that "decisions rendered by

---

[32] GATT, Art. XXIII, and discussion by Jackson, *The WTO*, p. 81.

[33] *Ibid.*, p. 85.

[34] DSU, Art. 21.1. For other clauses of the DSU pointing in the same direction, see further Jackson, *The WTO*, p. 88.

[35] *Ibid.*, pp. 85–87. See also Hélène Ruiz Fabri, "L'appel dans le règlement des différends de l'OMC: trois ans après, quinze rapports plus tard" 103 *Revue Générale de Droit International Public* (1999) 47–128; Edwin Vermulst, Petros C. Mavroidis and Paul Waer, "The functioning of the Appellate Body after four years: towards rule integrity" 33 *Journal of World Trade* (1999) 1–50.

[36] Florentino P. Feliciano, "Dispute settlement under the aegis of the World Trade Organization" in Antonio M. Elicaño, *Odyssey and Legacy: The Chief Justice Andrés R. Narvasa Centennial*

the Appellate Body are called 'Reports' rather than judgments" because they are made in the form of recommendations to the Dispute Settlement Body. However, upon "adoption by the DSB the decisions of the Appellate Body become binding upon the parties to the dispute. In other words, these decisions become *res judicata*."[37]

The judicial function of the WTO dispute settlement system has been strengthened in a number of other respects. The gradual resort to the rules of international law and to those governing the interpretation of treaties – a matter which under the GATT 1947 was not entirely accepted[38] – the clarification of the standards of review and their connection to national practice or decisions,[39] and the availability of procedures to deal with complaints about non-violation cases,[40] are all examples of how the system is developing towards an enhanced rule-oriented approach.[41] A proposal to establish a standing Panel Body that would perform the functions of a Court of First Instance, subject to the appeals procedure, has also been advanced.[42]

Notwithstanding this greater judicial emphasis, the system has not lost its flexibility and has not substituted for the role of governments in finding accommodations on the many issues where there can be differences of opinion. To this extent, the WTO dispute settlement system is genuinely at the service of the parties concerned. Through its contribution to dispute resolution it is also contributing to the development of free trade in the international community and to the attainment of the WTO's objectives.

Lecture Series (1998), pp. 179–202, lecture delivered on 12 November 1998, 192–193. See also Florentino P. Feliciano and Peter L.H. Van den Bossche, "The dispute settlement system of the World Trade Organization: institutions, process and practice" 75 *Philippine Law Journal* (2000) 1–46.

[37] Feliciano, "Dispute settlement," 197.

[38] See, e.g., *United States – Standards for Reformulated and Conventional Gasoline*, complaints by Venezuela (WT/DS2) and Brazil (WT/DS4), DSR 1996:I, and discussion by Jackson, *The WTO*, pp. 89, 94–95. See also James Cameron and Kevin R. Gray, "Principles of international law in the WTO Dispute Settlement Body" 50 *International and Comparative Law Quarterly* (2001) 248–298.

[39] Steven P. Croley and John H. Jackson, "WTO dispute procedures: standard of review, and deference to national governments" 90 *American Journal of International Law* (1996) 193.

[40] DSU, Art. 26, and discussion by Jackson, *The WTO*, pp. 92–93.

[41] *Ibid.*, pp. 89–97.

[42] European Communities, Discussion Paper on the Review of the Dispute Settlement Understanding (1999), as cited by Kim van der Borght in a review of the book by Palmeter and Mavroidis, *Dispute Settlement*, 94 *American Journal of International Law* (2000) 427–430, at 430, note 17.

Emergence of the individual in the WTO dispute settlement system

As the GATT 1947 and the WTO have been mainly concerned with the safeguard of treaty benefits accorded as between states,[43] the individual has had historically a marginal or non-existent role. But, as has been mentioned in the preceding chapters, in most cases it is the individual acting as a trader, investor or economic agent who has the greatest interest in the safeguarding of rights and who indeed suffers most in case of any impingement upon those rights. The prevalence of a market-oriented international system has brought the individual to the center stage of international economic relations, a trend which the WTO has not ignored and which will most probably inspire a number of additional developments in the future.

The GATT 1947 did not exclusively follow state related criteria for membership. It also accepted a "separate customs territory possessing full autonomy in the conduct of its external commercial relations" to be a party to the Agreement.[44] While this did not affect the status of the individual, it revealed that the arrangements under the GATT 1947 could eventually reach beyond the nation state. The fact that individuals had a prominent interest in trade benefits and rights was in many instances recognized at the national level.

This meant that in practice many of the cases brought under the GATT 1947 or the WTO have involved the interests of individuals and corporations that have been sponsored by their governments. The *Kodak-Fuji Film* case[45] is eloquent in this respect.[46] Moreover, on occasions the disputes coming before the WTO will have been previously discussed or investigated in domestic courts and procedures, where individuals will have a role of their own. However, this system is not really one of diplomatic protection before an international dispute settlement forum, nor is the exhaustion of domestic remedies a requirement to bring a case to the WTO.[47] It is rather an inter-state system that recognizes, albeit indirectly and subject to government support, the interests of individuals.

---

[43] Petersmann, "Dispute settlement system," 1241.
[44] GATT, Art. XII, and discussion by Jackson, *The WTO*, pp. 48–50.
[45] *Japan-Measures Affecting Consumer Photographic Film and Paper*, complaint by the United States, DSR 1998:IV.
[46] Thomas J. Schoenbaum, "WTO dispute settlement: praise and suggestions for reform" 47 *International and Comparative Law Quarterly* (1998) 647–658, at 656.
[47] Petersmann, "Dispute settlement system," 1240.

In areas where private rights are explicitly recognized under the WTO, the trend to accept a role for individuals will continue. Examples are the TRIPS Agreement in respect of intellectual property rights and the Agreement on Preshipment Inspection.[48] In particular, the latter allows for an independent review proceeding to which both exporters and inspection entities have access.

The decision of the Appellate Body in the *Bananas* case[49] has made an important contribution in this respect. First, the Appellate Body admitted a complaint by the USA against the European Community on import restraints on bananas, in spite of the claimant not being an exporter of this commodity.[50] The USA was making its claim on behalf of a major banana producer and an industrial association, which had initiated domestic action under section 301 of the United States Trade Act 1974 – an example of the close connection between such domestic proceedings and WTO claims.[51] The prevalence of private interests was influential in this decision, which also made a significant step in allowing a claimant to be represented by private counsel,[52] and did not exclude the possibility of private counsel preparing written pleadings and briefs or giving legal advice,[53] particularly when a participating state has limited capability of its own.

The DSU also provides a basis on which this development can to some extent be founded. A panel has the right to seek information and technical advice from "any individual or body which it deems appropriate."[54] It may also seek information from any relevant source and consult experts on given aspects of a case, including the request for an advisory report from an expert review group in factual, scientific or technical matters.[55] When information or advice is to be provided by individuals or bodies within the jurisdiction of a member, the panel will inform its authorities accordingly.

The WTO Agreement also authorizes the General Council to make arrangements for consultation and cooperation with non-governmental

---

[48] For a discussion of the TRIPS Agreement in this context, see *ibid.*, 1241. See also Art. 4 of the Agreement on Preshipment Inspection. See also Steve Charnovitz, "the WTO and the rights of the individual" 36 *Intereconomics* (2001) 98–108.

[49] *EC-Regime for the Importation, Sale and Distribution of Bananas*, complaints by Ecuador, Guatemala, Honduras, Mexico and the United States (WT/DS27), DSR 1997:II.

[50] *Ibid.*, 59–61, and discussion by Schoenbaum, "WTO dispute settlement," 653.

[51] Schoenbaum, "WTO dispute settlement," 654.

[52] *EC-Regime for the Importation, Sale and Distribution of Bananas*, complaints by Ecuador, Guatemala, Honduras, Mexico and the United States (WT/DS27), DSR 1997:II, p. 8, and discussion by Schoenbaum, "WTO dispute settlement," 655.

[53] Schoenbaum, "WTO dispute settlement," 655.

[54] DSU, Art. 13.1.   [55] DSU, Art. 13.2.

organizations concerned with matters within the scope of the Organization.[56] Some non-governmental organizations have strongly requested participation in WTO deliberations and panel proceedings, particularly by means of access to documentation and submission of *amicus curiae* briefs, and some arrangements have been made for the exchange of views and other forms of general consultation.[57] Moreover, the Appellate Body has clarified some important aspects relating to the submission of briefs, by holding in particular that panels may accept briefs from non-governmental sources even if these have not been requested and by permitting parties to include in their own submissions briefs prepared by non-governmental organizations.[58] The Appellate Body has asserted that briefs may also be accepted during the appeals procedure[59] and in one case issued procedural rules for such submissions.[60]

These developments have opened a new debate on which submissions may be regarded as pertinent, on the criteria for their selection and how to avoid discrimination against WTO members who are not entitled to submit their views unless acting as a party to the dispute.[61] While no doubt progress may also be expected in respect of the participation of non-governmental organizations in the framework of the WTO, the criteria described in other

---

[56] Marrakesh Agreement Establishing the World Trade Organization, Art. V, and discussion by Jackson, *The WTO*, p. 51.

[57] *Ibid.*, pp. 53–54.

[58] On the general question of briefs before panels see *United States–Import Prohibition of Certain Shrimp and Shrimp Products* (WT/DS58), DSR 1998:VIII, Appellate Body Report, para. 13, and comment by Julio Lacarte-Muró, "Developing countries and the WTO legal and dispute settlement system: a view from the bench," speech delivered to the UNCTAD Workshop on Settlement of Disputes in International Trade, Investment and Intellectual Property, Geneva, 20–22 January 2000, at 2. See also Jessica C. Pearlman, "Participation by private counsel in World Trade Organization dispute settlement proceedings" 30 *Law and Policy in International Business* (1999) 399–416; Nick Covelli, "Public international law and third party participation in WTO Panel proceedings" 33 *Journal of World Trade* (1999) 125–140.

[59] *United States – Imposition of Countervailing Duties on Certain Hot-Rolled Lead and Bismuth Carbon Steel Products Originating in the United Kingdom* (WT/DS138), reports adopted on 7 June 2000, Appellate Body report, paras. 36–42 with particular reference to the discussion on this question by the parties and other WTO members.

[60] *European Communities – Measures Affecting the Prohibition of Asbestos and Asbestos Products* (WT/DS 135), reports adopted on 5 April 2001, Appellate Body report, paras. 50–57.

[61] For a report on the debate ensuing the decision to admit *amicus* briefs, with particular reference to discussions at the Dispute Settlement Body, see "Bridges between trade and sustainable development," International Centre for Trade and Sustainable Development, June 2000, at 5, November-December 2000, at 4 and October 2002, at 15, with particular reference to the Appeals Body decision of 26 September 2002 on the *EC – Trade Description of Sardines* case.

chapters relating to the need to ensure professionalism, transparency and accountability of these organizations are also applicable here.[62]

A similar discussion about the submission of *amicus curiae* briefs has been held in the context of NAFTA. The arbitral tribunal in the *Methanex* case, operating under UNCITRAL Rules, decided that such briefs could be submitted in writing, subject to some procedural limitations.[63] Specific reference was made to the public policy issues involved in the matter under consideration.[64] It remains to be seen whether other tribunals will do the same.

WTO consultations, good offices, conciliation and mediation, as well as panel and Appellate Body proceedings[65] are subject to the requirements of confidentiality. Supposedly, arbitration should also be governed by a similar rule, though the procedure is to be mutually agreed by the parties. Strict approaches to confidentiality are justified in respect of arbitration and other dispute settlement arrangements that deal with normal trade and business matters. Recently, however, a different view has emerged in connection with arrangements that refer to trade and investment, and which relate to broader issues concerning public policies. Confidentiality in this other context has occasionally been criticized because it could conflict with transparency and the need to ensure that broader public interests are taken into account. This view has also been raised with respect to domestic proceedings.[66]

The experience of dispute settlement arrangements in many other areas has shown, however, that confidentiality is essential for the parties to come to an agreement or for the tribunal to reach a decision without the pressure of public opinion or other forms of interference in the course of settlement of a dispute. The professional competence of members of panels and the Appellate Body helps to ensure that issues concerning the interests of society will not be ignored under the blanket of confidentiality. This discussion, however, touches upon the question whether in cases involving public policy considerations a different standard of confidentiality should be applied to that applied in disputes of an ordinary commercial character.

A similar discussion on confidentiality has been undertaken in connection with the NAFTA arrangements. The notes on interpretation of some of

---

[62] See chapter 2, note 66 and associated text.
[63] *Methanex* v. *United States*, Order of the Tribunal, 15 January 2001.
[64] *Ibid.*, para. 49.   [65] DSU, Arts. 4.6, 5.6, 14.1, 17.10.
[66] Petersmann, "Dispute settlement system," 1204–1205, with reference at note 87 of Civil Action No. 92-0659 in the US District Court for the District of Columbia, *Public Citizen* v. *Office of the USTR*, Order of 6 November 1992.

NAFTA's Chapter 11 provisions recently adopted by the Free Trade Commission[67] record the agreement of the parties on the absence of a general duty of confidentiality. As a consequence, public access to the documents of a case is possible on the condition that confidential business information and some other privileged information is duly protected from disclosure.

In light of the above, the facilitation of access of individuals to the WTO dispute settlement system is likely to continue, perhaps along lines not dissimilar to those under the NAFTA or similar arrangements. The recognition of this reality is already underlying the whole approach to this system.[68]

It has been pointed out that the opening of the system to individuals could result in it being overloaded by private claims. To attend to this, it is argued, there would be a need to enlarge the panel system, to have full-time Appellate Body members and to strengthen the Secretariat, establishing in essence a court of international trade.[69] Many of these and other improvements are of course feasible and may be desirable, but the experience of ICSID and other specialized dispute settlement systems that allow for private claims shows that, while there is a gradual growth of submissions, this does not create an unmanageable situation.

Concern has also been expressed about the criteria according to which states could sponsor claimants,[70] in case this requirement is fulfilled. Here again, one may recall the precedents noted in prior chapters, in respect of the law of diplomatic protection and the current state of international practice. A separate dispute settlement forum for individual claims under the WTO has also been proposed.[71] In any event, to the extent that private claims might not require government sponsoring, there will still be a need for a screening procedure, perhaps linked to the Dispute Settlement Body. Only those claims involving a genuine merit and interest would be granted access to the dispute settlement arrangements under the WTO. Screening

---

[67] NAFTA Free Trade Commission, Notes of Interpretation of Certain Chapter 11 Provisions, 31 July 2001.

[68] Schoenbaum, "WTO dispute settlement," 655–658, with references at note 65 to discussions and proposals by Andrea Giardina and Americo Beviglia Zampetti, "Settling competition-related disputes: the arbitration alternative in the WTO framework" 31 *Journal of World Trade* (1997) 5–27; and Glen T. Schleyer, "Power to the people: allowing private parties to raise claims before the WTO dispute resolution system," *Fordham Law Review* (1997) 2275. See also Bernd-Roland Killmann, "The access of individuals to international trade dispute settlement" 13 *Journal of International Arbitration* (1996) 143–169; Patrick Specht, "The dispute settlement systems of WTO and NAFTA: analysis and comparison" 27 *Georgia Journal of International and Comparative Law* (1998) 57–138.

[69] Schoenbaum, "WTO dispute settlement," 655, 658.

[70] *Ibid.*, 655–656.   [71] *Ibid.*, 656.

arrangements have also been considered above in the discussion of the International Court of Justice.[72]

Specific arrangements to facilitate the access of individuals could be devised taking into account the experience of various existing dispute settlement systems, public and private. The important point, however, is to conceive a system which under the central guidance of the WTO would allow for diversified choices, ranging from alternative dispute resolution mechanisms to judicial determination. To some extent this is the approach already followed by the integrated WTO dispute settlement system, but if opened to individuals it might require a greater degree of decentralization. This is the point where a centralized system becomes structurally related to a decentralized alternative dispute resolution mechanism, which will be examined next as one of the likely features of dispute settlement in the international community at large.

[72] See chapter 2, note 72 and associated text, and also chapter 4, note 55 and associated text.

7

An alternative dispute resolution system
for international disputes

The public system of international adjudication performs an essential function in the settlement of disputes, both in inter-state relations and in a number of situations that involve individuals and other private parties. However, as has been shown in the preceding chapters, there is a constant need to facilitate dispute settlement in a broader context, particularly in so far as disputes increasingly involve private interests in a global market, regardless of whether states or other private parties are involved. This has led to the development of an alternative dispute resolution system for international disputes. This system is already one of the central features of international society and will no doubt be further developed in the years ahead. This chapter will examine some of the recent improvements in this field, explore some relevant domestic experiences and their possible influence on international developments, and present some proposals on how these developments might evolve into a structured system interconnected with public courts and tribunals.

Enhancement of an international alternative dispute resolution system

Alternative dispute resolution has been described in a domestic context as a halfway house between the certainty of the adversarial system and the flexibility of private negotiation.[1] But it does not exclude adjudication in its entirety. In fact, adjudication as a result of arbitration is very much a part

---

[1] George Applebey, "An overview of alternative dispute resolution" in Claude Samson and Jeremy McBride (eds.), *Alternative Dispute Resolution* (1993), pp. 26–41, at 37.

of the developing alternative dispute resolution system, as are decisions of a number of tribunals established for different specialized purposes. Only exceptionally has arbitration been excluded from alternative dispute settlement arrangements. The alternative envisaged is really in respect of the submission of a dispute to the ordinary courts of justice.[2] To this extent an alternative system involves some degree of perceived dissatisfaction with the courts' role in dispute settlement.

In fact, the goals of alternative dispute resolution in a domestic context confirm a certain degree of dissatisfaction with the performance of domestic courts. These goals are to pursue the relief of "court congestion, as well as undue cost and delay; to enhance community involvement in the dispute resolution process; to facilitate access to justice; and to provide more 'effective' dispute resolution."[3] The delay of courts in resolving cases, the complex and costly nature of adjudication and the lack of specialization to deal with new issues have often rendered formal adjudication inaccessible or ineffective.[4] Resort to alternative dispute resolution mechanisms domestically has many advantages as compared to ordinary court adjudication. However, there have also been important criticisms relating to the effects of privatization of justice, the lack of a scientific approach underlying some of these methods, the ambiguous character of hybrid techniques and the need for institutionalization and professionalism.[5]

When discussing international adjudication Bilder has rightly explained that in its traditional understanding this technique has some limitations.[6] For example, a party may be reluctant to entrust a third party with an important decision involving a win or lose result that is normally associated

---

[2] L. Neville Brown, "Alternative Dispute Resolution Tribunals" in Samson and McBride, *Alternative Dispute Resolution*, pp. 84–95, at 85.

[3] Applebey, "Overview," 27, with particular reference to Goldberg, Green and Sander, *Dispute Resolution* (1985).

[4] Applebey, "Overview," 30.

[5] Robert A. Baruch Bush, "Dispute resolution: the domestic arena – a survey of methods, applications, and critical issues" in John A. Vasquez, James Turner Johnson, Sanford Jaffe and Linda Stamato (eds.), *Beyond Confrontation: Learning Conflict Resolution in the Post-Cold War Era* (1998), pp. 9–37, at 23–27. See also generally Gordon R. Woodman, "The Alternative Law of Alternative Dispute Resolution" in Samson and McBride, *Alternative Dispute Resolution*, pp. 580–605; Louis Kriesberg, "Applications and misapplications of conflict resolution ideas to international conflicts" in Vasquez *et al.*, *Beyond Confrontation*, pp. 87–102; and John A. Vasquez, "The learning of peace: lessons from a multidisciplinary inquiry" in Vasquez *et al.*, *Beyond Confrontation*, pp. 211–238.

[6] Richard B. Bilder, "Some limitations of adjudication as an international dispute settlement technique" 23 *Virginia Journal of International Law* (1982) 1–12, at 2–3.

with judicial settlement. Other limitations relate to the fact that a decision may not always deal with the actual underlying causes of the dispute and the bad feeling caused by the efforts of one party to take another to court. The limited interest of states in having a court clarify or develop general rules of international law is also an obstacle in this respect.[7] As put by Reisman, adjudication is far from being the highest form of dispute resolution, as judicial romantics may believe: it is rather a sign of failure "for it signals that the parties have been unable to settle their differences amicably."[8]

The international system of alternative dispute settlement of today is very broad in scope. It includes the classic techniques of negotiation, consultation, conciliation, investigation and mediation, as well as arbitration generally and a variety of courts and tribunals established for the adjudication of specialized disputes. In fact, it could be said that it only excludes the International Court of Justice to the extent that this court is considered an ordinary court of law of the international community, in spite of its lack of effective compulsory jurisdiction.

But differently from the domestic experience, this international alternative system has not emerged as a result of dissatisfaction with the role of ordinary courts. In fact, the International Court of Justice has performed its tasks with dedication and expertise. The international alternative dispute resolution system came into being even before a standing international court of justice was established. The system has developed due to the need to safeguard freedom of choice, and due also to the broad availability of alternatives for settling disputes between states and other parties.

In spite of the differences, international alternative dispute resolution is acquiring an enhanced role as a consequence of realities that are not very different from those characterizing domestic developments in this field. The experience in the past century shows that states and other entities have a preference for solving their disputes by recourse to negotiations and other non-adversarial methods, while the judicial option is usually kept as an alternative of last resort. The traditional methods of judicial settlement have in many respects reached their limits in both the domestic and international ambits, requiring supplementary arrangements.

---

[7] *Ibid.*, 3–5.

[8] W. Michael Reisman, "The supervisory jurisdiction of the International Court of Justice: international arbitration and international adjudication" 258 *Recueil des Cours de l'Academie de Droit International* (1996) 9–394, at 383.

In fact, regardless of how the effectiveness of the International Court of Justice is assessed, it is evident that disputes concerning trade, investments and economic relations generally are not brought before this court. These disputes are the most common for the settlement of which the international community has sought and found alternative arrangements. The most relevant of those were examined in preceding chapters.

Another factor encouraging alternative arrangements is the need of contemporary dispute settlement to ensure prevention rather than resolution of disputes, an objective which often may only be achieved by means of new mechanisms.[9] The emphasis on prevention is relevant with respect to both political and legal disputes, and it affects both state and non-state actors. Recent experiences relating to peace-keeping, peace-building and peace-making, together with the intensification of monitoring techniques and other elements associated with these efforts, are important indicators of the latter. The same applies to corporate dispute management, which is orientated to ensure both prevention and the safeguarding of good relations between corporate entities. This approach will become paramount in the following years, although of course formal dispute settlement will always need to be available in case the preventive efforts fail.

As a result of the emphasis on prevention in the legal environment (which is likely to reduce the legal risks involved),[10] and of the availability of formal procedures to this effect, a significant increase in the number of disputes submitted to prevention and resolution may be expected. Furthermore, just as the exclusion of disputes affecting "vital interests" was subsumed in the traditional distinction between legal and non-legal disputes,[11] so the theoretical line separating legal from political disputes will continue to fade, if it ever was clear. This will result in increasing the types of disputes submitted to such arrangements. It will also result in new pressures on enlarging the availability of dispute settlement options.

Two other positive consequences may be expected. First, a greater institutionalization of dispute settlement should occur, in order to handle the

---

[9] Ibrahim F.I. Shihata, "Implementation, enforcement and compliance with international environmental agreements: practical suggestions in light of the World Bank's experience" 9 *Georgetown International Environmental Law Review* (1996) 37–51.

[10] George W. Coombe, "The future: implementing new approaches to the settlement of transnational commercial disputes" 17 *Canada-United States Law Journal* (1991) 533–590, at 535.

[11] Christine Gray and Benedict Kingsbury, "Developments in dispute settlement: inter-state arbitration since 1945," *British Year Book of International Law* (1992) 97–134, at 103.

new functions and volumes involved. Second, dispute settlement will be increasingly governed by rules of law rather than by political considerations, as in the past.[12]

The above-mentioned prevalence of market economies[13] will increasingly have a strong influence on the development of alternative dispute settlement. The direct and expeditious access of individuals to the settlement of disputes with other entities, whether state or non-state, will be a requirement that the system has to satisfy efficiently. The fact that private property and individual rights are today essential elements of the liberal democratic state,[14] and are also affecting the structure of the international society, means that individuals will expect effective protection in terms of both equality under the law and control of arbitrariness. The rule of law thus becomes a key factor in ensuring the climate of stability and predictability required by the adequate functioning of a market economy.[15]

The dispute settlement demands of an international society based on market economy and the increasing role of individuals is leading to various innovative arrangements, as well as to certain forms of privatization of international justice.[16] While the techniques used by international law in this respect are not new, their scope is rapidly changing, and a number of alternatives have been introduced. In order to meet these new demands dispute settlement bodies should play a creative role when clarifying the meaning of rules that are not always clear or precise.[17] This task will require more stringent standards relating to the independence and qualification of lawyers and professionals involved in dispute settlement, and a greater institutionalization of the procedures followed. In this respect, institutionalization and professionalism will be important issues that the system must address, to avoid the criticism that has been made with respect to parallel developments in the domestic scenario.

---

[12] *Ibid.*, 103.

[13] Ibrahim F.I. Shihata, *Complementary Reform* (1997), ch. 2, "Settlement of disputes," pp. 31–53, at 33.

[14] Daniel S. Sullivan, "Effective international dispute settlement mechanisms and the necessary condition of liberal democracy" 81 *Georgetown Law Journal* (1993) 2369–2412, at 2373.

[15] Shihata, *Complementary Reform*, p. 34.

[16] *Ibid.*, p. 44, with reference to J.B. Weinstein, "Some benefits and risks of privatization of justice through ADR" 11 *Ohio State Journal on Dispute Resolution* (1996) 241; see also Malcolm Richard Wilkey, "International trade and foreign direct investment" 26 *Law and Policy in International Business* (1995) 613–631, at 615.

[17] Shihata, *Complementary Reform*, p. 36.

Perfecting traditional mechanisms of alternative dispute settlement under international law

The evolution of alternative dispute resolution in international law throughout the twentieth century has been examined in a recent study[18] and will not be discussed here. However, it is important to underline that the mechanisms of alternative dispute resolution have played a far more important role in the actual settlement of disputes than the International Court of Justice. This may be seen in particular when the utilization of arbitration is examined. Conciliation and mediation have not been used massively but have performed an important role in this field. Another point to be noted is that these alternative methods have been much perfected in recent years, as will be summarized below.

From negotiations to consultations

While at first sight it would appear that, in view of their simplicity, negotiations and consultations are an ordinary occurrence, this is not always the case. In fact, occasionally negotiations and consultations are difficult to engage in because of the unwillingness of the complainant to start a procedure that could lead to a compromise solution or another type of commitment. A first step to perfect this mechanism is to develop the requirement of notification of actions that are likely to affect the rights of other parties,[19] and eventually to associate other interested states with the domestic decision-making process that is likely to have such an effect.[20] A second step is the broader undertaking of consultations so as to prevent the emergence of a dispute or ensure its early solution.[21] To refrain from actions likely to

---

[18] See Francisco Orrego Vicuña and Christopher Pinto, *The Peaceful Settlement of Disputes: Prospects for the Twenty-First Century*, Final Report for the Centennial Commemoration of the First Peace Conference, May 1999, published in F. Kalhoven (ed.), *The Centennial of the First Peace Conference* (2000), p. 388.

[19] See, e.g., the Canada-United States Free Trade Agreement, 22–23 December 1987 and 2 January 1988, (1988) 27 *International Legal Materials* 281, Art. 1803, and comments by Louis B. Sohn, "Bipartite consultative commissions for preventing and resolving disputes relating to international trade treaties" in *International Law in an Evolving World, Liber Amicorum Eduardo Jiménez de Aréchaga* (1994), pp. 1181–1200, at 1183.

[20] Institut de Droit International, Resolution on Responsibility and Liability under International Law for Environmental Damage, Art. 29, Session de Strasbourg, 4 September 1997 (1998) 37 *International Legal Materials* 1473.

[21] OSCE, Convention on Conciliation and Arbitration in the Framework of the OSCE, 15 December 1992, (1993) 32 *International Legal Materials* 557 (hereinafter cited as "OSCE, Convention "), Preamble; see in particular the Principles adopted by CSCE at La Valette,

aggravate the situation and eventually to adopt interim measures would supplement this approach.[22]

In view of the preventive function of these methods, other related steps might also be considered. The usefulness of monitoring of situations that might result in disputes has been emphasized lately in the context of political affairs,[23] but it may be equally recommended in other types of public and private relations, including questions of compliance.[24] Availability of information becomes a particularly important requirement in this respect.[25]

Given the increasingly greater complexity of these arrangements, institutionalization of procedures will necessarily follow.[26] The prominent role performed in the past by bilateral commissions[27] is being supplemented by the action of regional and global international organizations. A United Nations agreement on consultations has been proposed to facilitate the operation of this particular method.[28] The obligations relating to negotiations might be strengthened first by becoming a general principle of international law, but this could be done even more effectively through more specific international regimes on settlement of disputes.

Institutionalized inquiry

The role of inquiry has also been enhanced lately as a result of the need to obtain information associated with the prevention and settlement of

---

8 February 1991, and the principle on prevention of disputes; and comments by Sohn, "Bipartite consultative commissions," 1184–1185.

[22] OSCE, Convention, Art. 16; see also North American Free Trade Agreement (NAFTA), 17 December 1992 (1993) 32 *International Legal Materials* 694, Art. 2006; and comments by Sohn, "Bipartite consultative commissions," 1183–1185.

[23] United Nations Secretary-General, *An Agenda for Peace: Preventive Diplomacy, Peacemaking and Peace-keeping*, UN Doc. S/24111 (1992), para. 27.

[24] Institut de Droit International, Resolution on Procedure for the Adoption and Implementation of Rules in the Field of the Environment, Session de Strasbourg, 4 September 1997, 67–II *Annuaire de l'Institut de Droit International* (1998) 514.

[25] NAFTA, Art. 2006, and comments by Sohn, "Bipartite consultative commissions," 1184.

[26] *Ibid.*, 1196–1197.   [27] *Ibid.*, 1189.

[28] Louis B. Sohn, *The Use of Consultations for Monitoring Compliance with Agreements Concluded under the Auspices of International Organizations* (1993), pp. 80–82. See also the extensive discussion on settlement of disputes in the context of the Manila Declaration on the Peaceful Settlement of International Disputes adopted by the United Nations General Assembly in November 1992, 19 *United Nations Chronicle* (December 1982) 80–81; and comments by Louis B. Sohn, "Draft General Treaty on the Peaceful Settlement of International Disputes: a proposal and report," American Bar Association, Committee on World Order Under Law, 20 *The International Lawyer* (1986) 261–291, at 261.

disputes. This classic method has proven to be particularly helpful in dealing with highly technical disputes where the facts need to be clearly established and understood. However, the new demands of international society have evidenced the need for innovation in this method. Like other methods, institutionalization of inquiry has been significantly developed and this will no doubt be an essential feature of its further evolution. Important steps have been taken in this respect by the Security Council as far as peace and security are concerned,[29] and by a number of technical organizations, notably the GATT 1947 and the World Trade Organization.[30] The Permanent Court of Arbitration has also prepared Optional Rules for fact-finding commissions of inquiry.[31] The traditional model of bilateral commissions of inquiry continues to have a useful role.[32]

Conciliation and its links

Conciliation has been well developed under international law since the period 1899–1907 and innovations are introduced from time to time, as demand for this option is maintained. An interesting example of current trends is provided by the 1992 Convention on Conciliation and Arbitration of the Organization for Security and Cooperation in Europe.[33] It shows the process of institutionalization, not by the intervention of standing bodies but, as in the case of the Permanent Court of Arbitration, by the availability of a roster of conciliators and arbitrators,[34] which is a more effective alternative.

Another important feature of conciliation is that it is usually linked with other options, including arbitration. The role of good offices should also be considered in this context. The OSCE Convention develops the principle of subsidiarity so as not to impair the jurisdiction of the International Court of Justice, the Permanent Court of Arbitration and the major European

---

[29] Louis B. Sohn, *Broadening the Role of the United Nations in Preventing, Mitigating or Ending International or Internal Conflicts that Threaten International Peace and Security*, International Rule of Law Center Occasional Papers, Second Series, No. 1 (1997), p. 35.

[30] See generally chapter 4.

[31] PCA Optional Rules of Procedure for Fact-finding Commissions of Inquiry, 1997.

[32] See, e.g., the Chile-United States Treaty for the Settlement of Disputes of 1914.

[33] OSCE, Convention, and comments by Laurence Cuny, *L'OSCE et le Règlement Pacifique des Différends: La Cour de Conciliation et d'Arbitrage* (IHEI, 1997); Lucius Caflisch, "Vers des mécanismes pan-européens de règlement pacifique des différends" 97 *Revue Générale de Droit International Public* (1993), 1–36.

[34] OSCE, Convention, Art. 3.

courts.[35] This is an important principle which provides for a hierarchy in dispute settlement methods or jurisdictions.

Compulsory recourse to conciliation has been an important feature of dispute settlement found in both bilateral[36] and multilateral treaties.[37] Other interesting innovations concerning conciliation are provided by the practice of the Chile–United States Commission for the Settlement of Disputes, operating on the basis of the only treaty of the Bryan network that has ever been invoked.[38] This is in essence a commission of inquiry and conciliation, with a possibility of arbitration subject to some complex requirements. By virtue of an *ad hoc* agreement the Commission was entrusted with the mandate to arrive at binding decisions on compensation, which transformed it for this purpose into an adjudicatory body.[39] Such developments evidence quite vividly that even old treaties and mechanisms might be put to an entirely new use in the context of changing international relations and needs.

Truth and Reconciliation as a new alternative

Many international disputes originate in situations of internal conflict that subsequently become, directly or indirectly, internationalized. New approaches to deal with such internal conflicts have recently been developed. They sometimes interrelate with, or have implications for, dispute settlement under international law or other arrangements. The model of a Truth and Reconciliation Commission followed by both Chile and South Africa, as well as by other countries, in connection with their respective transitions to democracy, are recent examples.

The establishment of International Truth and Reconciliation Commissions might prove an adequate alternative in some situations, particularly where the important issue is to set a truthful historical record of events and responsibilities that may lead to conciliation, and not that of punishing

---

[35] *Ibid.*, Art. 19, and comments by Lucius Caflisch and Laurence Cuny, "La Cour de Conciliation et d'Arbitrage de l'OSCE: problèmes d'actualité," *OSZE Jahrbuch* (1997) 4.

[36] Chile-Argentina, Treaty of Peace and Friendship, 29 November 1984, Annex 1, Art. 2, (1985) 24 *International Legal Materials* 11.

[37] United Nations Convention on the Law of the Sea, Art. 284; OSCE, Convention, Art. 18.

[38] Chile-United States Treaty for the Settlement of Disputes of 1914; Commission decision in the matter of compensation for the deaths of Letelier and Moffitt, (1992) 31 *International Legal Materials* 1; and comments by Gray and Kingsbury, "Developments," 100, note 17.

[39] Chile-United States, Agreement to Settle Dispute Concerning Compensation for the Deaths of Letelier and Moffitt, (1991) 30 *International Legal Materials* 422.

individuals. This new alternative mechanism has the advantage of always respecting the traditions and specific circumstances of national societies involved in such conflicts. It will not result in the application of views or values that are often alien to such realities. Generally, there is a need to harmonize alternative dispute resolution mechanisms with the realities of local cultures.[40]

Flexible mediation

Mediation has followed an evolution similar to conciliation and has proven to be a method in growing demand under domestic arrangements. Unlike conciliation, however, where there are usually no suggestions of specific terms of settlement, the mediator usually puts forward recommendations to settle the dispute.[41] The parties are free to accept or not accept such proposals, but on occasion they would prefer to avoid any element in the process that might constitute a precedent or affect the desired flexibility. The barring of later use in adjudication of confidential information submitted in the process has been identified as an important element to this end.[42]

This is why key examples of mediation, in particular the Papal mediation between Chile and Argentina,[43] have proceeded with great flexibility, and resulted in suggestions to the parties when the mediator has deemed it useful, also helping the parties to negotiate directly under the guidance of the mediator. In fact, there is here a practical combination of both mediation and conciliation, which is the feature likely to predominate in the future.

The essential feature of mediation or other third party intervention will be to appoint in this capacity an individual, commission or institution that the parties are prepared to trust.[44] This fact explains the increasing institutionalization of these procedures in regional or global organizations.[45] It has been suggested that dispute settlement mechanisms should have an intermediary to bring the parties together and encourage them to choose

---

[40] Woodman, "Alternative Law," 600.

[41] Howard M. Holtzmann, "Dispute resolution in Europe under the UNCITRAL conciliation rules" in Daniel Bardonnet (ed.), *Le Règlement Pacifique des Différends Internationaux en Europe: Perspectives d'Avenir* (Colloque de l'Académie de Droit International, 1991), pp. 293–303, at 297–298.

[42] *Ibid.*, pp. 302–303.

[43] Santiago Benadava, "La mediación de la Santa Sede en el diferendo chileno-argentino sobre la zona austral" in *International Law at a Time of Perplexity: Essays in Honour of Shabtai Rosenne* (1989), pp. 33–50.

[44] J.G. Merrills, *International Dispute Settlement* (1998), p. 286.

[45] Holtzmann, "Dispute resolution," 303.

a mode for settling their dispute without waiting for the parties to take the initiative. This approach envisages a special proactive role for mediation.[46]

Alternative uses of existing facilities

The relevance of the methods discussed above in contemporary dispute settlement is further evidenced by the continuing adaptation of the available rules and facilities for the purpose of dispute settlement. Examples of this, also occuring in specialized areas, include the following: the 1950 Revised General Act for the Pacific Settlement of International Disputes,[47] the 1980 UNCITRAL Conciliation Rules, the 1988 Rules of Conciliation of the International Chamber of Commerce (merged in 2001 into the new Amicable Dispute Resolution system), the 1995 United Nations Model Rules for the Conciliation of Disputes between States and the 1996 Permanent Court of Arbitration Optional Conciliation Rules.[48]

In spite of the fact that conciliation was not included in either the 1899 or 1907 Conventions, the Permanent Court of Arbitration developed a practice allowing for such procedure[49] and has succeeded in establishing the rules noted above. The fact that facilities have been made available to both international organizations and private parties is a significant indication of the current evolution in dispute settlement[50] and updates the Conventions in a practical manner, without requiring formal amendment.[51] It is also an important precedent as how to update treaty arrangements that have fallen behind time, as has happened rather dramatically in the Inter-American System.[52]

Expanding the role of technical bodies

The use of inquiry, conciliation and mediation in the context of technical bodies has also been a most successful experience in the "reference" procedure established under the 1909 Boundary Waters Treaty between Great

---

[46] Comments on Orrego Vicuña and Pinto, Report, 1999, by Mr. Roy S. Lee, 30 November 1998, at 1–2.

[47] See discussion by Holtzmann, "Dispute resolution," 297–298.

[48] Permanent Court of Arbitration, 1999 Steering Committee, *Final Report and Recommendations to the Administrative Council* (June 1997), pp. 4, 13.

[49] *Ibid.*, pp. 12–14.   [50] *Ibid.*, pp. 10–12.   [51] *Ibid.*, pp. 6–7.

[52] On the settlement of disputes in the Inter-American system, with particular reference to the 1948 Pact of Bogotá, see generally F.V. Garcia Amador, *The Inter-American System* (1983).

Britain (now Canada) and the USA.[53] With the consent of both parties a dispute may be formally referred to the International Joint Commission, and if this body is unable to decide the matter the case is then submitted to an umpire.[54] However, under a more practical approach either party may also bring a question or difference to the Commission, which may issue a report and recommendations, relying on factual inquiries by experts and other arrangements.[55] This constitutes a combination of formal dispute settlement, eventually leading to arbitration, with more flexible arrangements, which allow for inquiry, as well as certain types of conciliation and mediation.

This approach is most appropriate for dispute settlement in specialized areas of cooperation, and this or a similar combination of methods should be particularly encouraged in future bilateral or multilateral arrangements of the kind. Expert determination has also become a normal feature of key international dispute settlement arrangements between private entities, such as the International Chamber of Commerce.

Enlarging the facilities for international arbitration

As has been noted above, alternative dispute resolution methods do not normally exclude adjudication by way of arbitration or courts and tribunals that might be established to provide for alternative or specialized arrangements. International arbitration, whether for public, private or mixed disputes, has been one of the most notable developments of dispute settlement in the past century and is likely to continue being used to its full capacity in the present one. The main trends currently characterizing international arbitration have been pointed out below.

Consent in submitting disputes to arbitration

As international arbitration is the oldest and perhaps best established method for the settlement of disputes under international law, it will remain

---

[53] United States-Great Britain, Treaty Relating to Boundary Waters, and Questions Arising Between the United States and Canada, 11 January 1909, 36 Stat. 2448, T.S. No. 548; and see Great Lakes Water Quality Agreement of 1972, 23 U.S.T. 301, T.I.A.S. No. 7312, and Great Lakes Water Quality Agreement of 1978, 30 U.S.T. 1383, T.I.A.S. No. 9257.

[54] Edith Brown Weiss, "Managing international water conflicts: the Great Lakes (USA-Canada)" (unpublished paper, February 1997), pp. 1–2.

[55] *Ibid.*, 1–2; see also Edith Brown Weiss, "New directions for the Great Lakes Water Quality Agreement: a commentary" 65 *Chicago-Kent Law Review* (1989) 375–386.

a viable alternative to judicial settlement in the future.[56] However, as with judicial settlement, it is not to be expected that a truly compulsory jurisdiction of arbitral tribunals will be any more acceptable than in the past with respect to disputes relating to general rules or issues of international law.[57] Arbitral jurisdiction will continue to be built on the consensual acceptance of the parties, given on an *ad hoc* basis or in anticipation of a dispute by means of an optional clause.[58]

Perfecting arbitral arrangements

In spite of the latter general limitation, progress is expected in a number of other aspects. First, compulsory jurisdiction is finding increasing application in specialized and technical matters.[59] Second, the possibility of preparing lists of subjects in respect of which arbitration might be obligatory continue to attract authors, just as was proposed in the 1899–1907 negotiations.[60] This approach could well be linked not to general questions of international law, but to the specialized fields in which it could better prosper. Third, general clauses for the exclusion of arbitration in respect of certain categories of disputes are either obsolete or fading away.[61] And fourth, as with other methods, increasing institutionalization will continue to develop so as to make this alternative more effective.

Surmounting legal difficulties

A number of legal problems that have haunted arbitration in the past might find prospective solutions in this new context. The discussion about arbitrability and the existence or non-existence of a dispute that has often been raised in connection with arbitration,[62] could in itself be submitted to a

---

[56] Gray and Kingsbury, "Developments," 109.

[57] *Ibid.*, 109. See also generally M.C.W. Pinto, "Structure, process, outcome: thoughts on the 'essence' of international arbitration" 6 *Leyden Journal of International Law* (1993) 241–264.

[58] Institut de Droit International, Projet de règlement pour la procédure arbitrale internationale, 1875, and discussion by Santiago Torres Bernárdez, "L'arbitrage interétatique" in Bardonnet, *Règlement Pacifique*, pp. 205–267, at 213–214. With respect to the OSCE Convention, see also Cuny, L'OSCE, pp. 68–69.

[59] Torres Bernárdez, "L'arbitrage interétatique," 263.

[60] James Brown Scott, *The Reports of the Hague Conferences of 1899 and 1907* (1917), pp. 60–61, at 392–393; Sohn, "Draft General Treaty," 282–284; Torres Bernárdez, "L'arbitrage interétatique," 263–264.

[61] See note 11 and associated text.

[62] Torres Bernárdez, "L'arbitrage interétatique," 222–223.

decision by an independent body or authority in the context of institution-alized proceedings. A particular role in this respect could be envisaged for the President of the International Court of Justice.

The increasing recourse to international law as the law applicable in arbitration will significantly facilitate the task of tribunals in identifying the general or specialized governing rules, including the role of equity as a principle of international law and, where appropriate, the right to decide *ex aequo et bono*. It is of interest to note that in the 1957 European Conven-tion an arbitral decision may be adopted *ex aequo et bono* in the silence of a *compromis* or in absence thereof, but with the added safeguard of the obliga-tion to take into account the general principles of international law and to respect conventional commitments and international decisions binding the parties.[63] It is a kind of international law, governed by the *ex aequo et bono* principle, that may provide the necessary flexibility within legal limits.

Problems relating to the compliance with arbitral awards may also be addressed in the framework of institutionalized proceedings. This is no longer a question to be left solely to the good faith and honor of the par-ties[64] and measures related to domestic enforcement and other aspects of implementation will need to be established. The experience of the ICSID Convention in respect of the enforcement of arbitral awards is particu-larly valuable in this context.[65] The improvement of the mechanism of the 1958 New York Convention[66] is also likely, with the objective of reaching agreement on the global enforcement of arbitral awards.

Institutionalized arbitration in the Permanent Court of Arbitration

The process of institutionalization offers interesting opportunities for the Permanent Court of Arbitration, for both inter-state arbitration under the Hague Conventions and other relevant participants. The 1992 Optional Rules for arbitration between two states and the 1993 Optional Rules

---

[63] European Convention for the Peaceful Settlement of Disputes of 29 April 1957, Art. 26; and comments by Torres Bernárdez, "L'arbitrage interétatique," 247–248.
[64] *Ibid.*, 251–252.
[65] See chapter 5, note 21 and associated text.
[66] Convention on the Recognition and Enforcement of Foreign Arbitral Awards, New York 1958. See also the 1975 Inter-American Convention on International Commercial Arbitration, the 1979 Inter-American Convention on Extra-territorial Validity of For-eign Judgments and Arbitral Awards and the 1983 Convention on Judicial Cooperation between Members of the Arab League, and discussion in International Law Association, Committee on International Commercial Arbitration, *Public Policy as a Ground for Refusing Enforcement of Foreign Arbitral Awards*, report by Audley Sheppard (1998), pp. 5–7.

established for arbitration between two parties of which only one is a state (like those adopted in 1996 for arbitration involving international organizations and states and for arbitration between international organizations and private parties and those adopted in 2001 for the arbitration of disputes relating to natural resources and the environment)[67] illustrate well the link between this system of arbitration and the new trends in the field.

In addition, the PCA could perform useful functions in respect of many regional arbitration systems that lack adequate institutional support. This is the case, for example, of the 1948 Pact of Bogotá in the ambit of the Organization of American States or the 1964 Organization of African Unity Protocol on mediation, conciliation and arbitration.[68] In such situations the PCA would not replace the regional organizations but would supplement their functions as needed. Similar roles could be performed in the context of various United Nations resolutions on arbitration or other treaties.

Fast-track arbitration

A recent important trend is the establishment of fast-track forms of arbitration, aimed at achieving results in a short time-frame and lowering the costs and difficulties associated with traditional arbitration. In 1978 the International Chamber of Commerce established a Standing Committee for the Regulation of Contractual Relations. Its aim was to make recommendations that the parties undertook to consider in good faith or adopt decisions that the parties agreed to respect, as if they were contractual provisions in spite of not taking the form of an award.[69] In 1990 the International Chamber of Commerce adopted a pre-arbitral referee procedure to remedy the problems caused by slow arbitration procedures.[70] Although these initiatives have not been successful, they indicate a need to be addressed by international arbitration. Fast-track arbitration has been also successfully

---

[67] Permanent Court of Arbitration, 1999 Steering Committee, *Final Report and Recommendations to the Administrative Council* (June 1997), pp. 10–12. See also generally International Bureau of the Permanent Court of Arbitration, *International Alternative Dispute Resolution: Past, Present and Future* (2000). See also Optional Rules for Arbitration of Disputes Relating to Natural Resources and/or the Environment, 19 June 2001.

[68] For a reference to regional and other relevant arbitration treaties, see Torres Bernárdez, "L'arbitrage interétatique," 209–210.

[69] Jan Paulsson, "Fast-Track arbitration in Europe (with special reference to the WIPO Expedited Arbitration Rules)" 18 *Hastings International and Comparative Law Review* (1995) 713–717, at 714.

[70] *Ibid.*, 714.

conducted under the normal rules of arbitration of the International Chamber of Commerce.[71]

A promising mechanism of this kind has been established by the World Intellectual Property Organization in terms of Expedited Arbitration Rules, which simplify the Arbitration Rules of this Organization[72] in order to attain a faster result. The key elements of the expedited mechanism are the appointment of a sole arbitrator and the streamlining of deadlines throughout the procedure. Mediation, eventually followed by arbitration, is also available.[73] Alternative mechanisms are also available for the resolution of disputes on Internet domain names.[74] As noted above, expeditious arbitration under the Dispute Settlement Understanding is now also available in the WTO.

Significant experience of international private arbitration

The development of private commercial arbitration has had an important effect on the improvement of arbitration mechanisms generally and on consolidating this ancient form of alternative dispute resolution. Many of the mechanisms discussed above are directly or indirectly related to private arbitration arrangements or to other such arrangements that apply to any kind of dispute, whether private, public or mixed. One of the most successful experiences in this field has been that of the Arbitration Rules adopted by the United Nations Commission on International Trade Law (UNCITRAL) in 1976[75] and the related 1985 Model Law.[76]

---

[71] *Ibid.*, 717.

[72] WIPO Arbitration Rules and Expedited Arbitration Rules, 1995, (1995) 34 *International Legal Materials* 559.

[73] WIPO Mediation Rules, 1995. The dispute settlement process is under the management of the WIPO Arbitration and Mediation Center established in 1994. See generally C.C. Fernandez and J. Spolter, "International intellectual property dispute resolution: is mediation a sleeping giant?" 53 *Dispute Resolution Journal* (1998) 62–69.

[74] Ernst-Ulrich Petersmann, "Alternative dispute settlement in international trade, investment and intellectual property law: an overview," UNCTAD Workshop on Settlement of Disputes in International Trade, Investment and Intellectual Property, 20–22 January 2000, at 23.

[75] UNCITRAL Arbitration Rules, 1976. For a discussion of alternative dispute resolution and litigation, see Margaret Wang, "Are alternative dispute resolution methods superior to litigation in resolving disputes in international commerce?" 16 *Arbitration International* (2000) 189–211. See also Stephen M. Schwebel, *International Arbitration: Three Salient Problems* (1987); Martin Hunter, "International commercial dispute resolution: the challenge of the twenty-first century" 16 *Arbitration International* (2000) 379–392.

[76] United Nations General Assembly Resolution 40/72, 11 December 1985. See Howard M. Holtzmann, *A Guide to the UNCITRAL Model Law on International Commercial Arbitration: Legislative History and Commentary* (1988).

Major international arbitration centres provide services for the settlement of commercial and other disputes, frequently facilitating conciliation or mediation. An example of this institutional development are the Rules of Arbitration and the Rules of Amicable Dispute Resolution of the International Chamber of Commerce.[77] Arrangements for the provision of such services have been established regionally, (for example, the Inter-American Commercial Arbitration Commission)[78] or have been devised to operate in conjunction with major trade agreements, as is the case of the Commercial Arbitration and Mediation Center of the Americas that aims to provide these services particularly in the context of the North American Free Trade Agreement (NAFTA).[79]

National centers of this kind also provide important facilities for dispute settlement, often acquiring a significant international dimension. An example is the American Arbitration Association, which makes available International Arbitration Rules, Procedures for Cases under UNCITRAL Arbitration Rules, Commercial Arbitration Rules, Commercial Mediation Rules, Patent Arbitration Rules, Commercial Financial Transactions Arbitration Rules and Construction Industry Arbitration Rules.[80] Similarly, the Center for Public Resources Institute for Dispute Resolution, established in New York, makes available a Model Mediation Procedure for Business Disputes in the United States and Canada, a Model Procedure for Mediation of Business Disputes in Europe, CPR Non-Administered Arbitration Rules and CPR Non-Administered International Arbitration Rules.[81]

The London Court of International Arbitration is another major international center, facilitating resort to Arbitration Rules and a Mediation Procedure.[82] Another example is the International Arbitration Institute in Paris. Santiago, Singapore, Stockholm and other cities offer such services for

---

[77] The Rules of Arbitration became effective 1 January 1998, (1997) 36 *International Legal Materials* 1604. The ICC ADR Rules became effective 1 July 2001.

[78] See generally the Inter-American Convention on International Commercial Arbitration, 1975.

[79] Commercial Arbitration and Mediation Center of the Americas, Arbitration Rules, Mediation Rules, 15 March 1996, (1996) 35 *International Legal Materials* 1541. In respect of an initiative for ASEAN see Pearlie M.C. Koh, "Enhancing economic co-operation: a regional arbitration centre for ASEAN?" 49 *International and Comparative Law Quarterly* (2000) 390–412. See also M.I.M. Aboul Enein, "Arbitration under the auspices of the Cairo Regional Center for Commercial Arbitration" 2 *Journal of International Arbitration* (1985) 23–44.

[80] For sources and texts see www.internationaladr.com   [81] *Ibid.*

[82] *Ibid.* See also the City Disputes Panel, that offers dispute settlement services to a variety of sectors of private business.

the benefit of trade and industry.[83] Regular joint meetings of the American Arbitration Association, the International Chamber of Commerce and the International Centre for the Settlement of Investment Disputes provide a useful opportunity to compare experiences and discuss new problems and issues in international arbitration and alternative dispute resolution.

Expert determination has also in many respects become intertwined with arbitration and should be regarded as supplementary. A number of the centers described offer such expert services. On occasions expert determination is turned into an award or an enforceable contract. In other instances experts integrate the arbitration tribunal or provide advice to it. Approaches such as Dispute Review Boards and Dispute Adjudication Boards also involve a high degree of expertise.

A successful experience of expert integration has been undertaken in some UNCC panels. One particularly interesting outcome of this approach has been the development of an alternative valuation methodology when in the circumstances of a claim the normal methodology envisaged proved to be entirely inappropriate.[84]

Diminishing the costs of international arbitration and other procedures

The costs of arbitration, judicial settlement and other procedures have often deterred the recourse to international dispute settlement. This is a concern particularly in the context of a globalized economy where there is active participation of states, large and small corporations, individual traders and investors and ordinary citizens. For many of these entities costs could be prohibitive. A Fund established by the Permanent Court of Arbitration, from which a substantial part of such expenditures might be reimbursed to qualifying states, aims at facilitating recourse to arbitration under the auspices of that body.[85] Similarly, in 1989 the United Nations established a Trust Fund financed through voluntary contributions, to assist states in the

---

[83] For national facilities offering arbitration and mediation services see generally the listing at www.internationaladr.com

[84] United Nations Compensation Commission, *First Report and Recommendations of the F/2 Panel* (1999).

[85] For information on the operation of the Fund, see 94th *Annual Report of the Permanent Court of Arbitration* (1996), paras. 2–4, 53 and Annex 10. See also the report of a meeting (London, 31 January–1 February 1997) on Funding of and Access to International Courts and Dispute Settlement Bodies, organized jointly by the Programme on International Law and Sustainable Development of the Foundation for International Environmental Law and Development (FIELD) and the Center on International Co-operation, New York University.

settlement of disputes through the International Court of Justice.[86] These initiatives might in due course reach beyond states and include other participants in the dispute settlement process. A suggestion for an international small claims procedure and other arrangements will be discussed below.

Domestic alternative dispute resolution: some experiences relevant to international dispute settlement

Alternative dispute resolution has become a favored approach to dispute settlement in the USA in the past twenty-five years and, more recently, in the United Kingdom and other countries.[87] Besides the classic methods of negotiation, conciliation, mediation and arbitration, alternative dispute resolution includes a variety of other methods developed in the context of those domestic experiences.

Among these alternatives is court-ordered arbitration. Here, an ordinary court of law will appoint an arbitrator who will conduct proceedings and deliver an award. This award can be rejected by either party and, if so, the case will continue in the original court. If the award is not rejected, it then becomes final and binding. Non-binding arbitration involves a decision that is not binding on the parties but is helpful in reaching a negotiated settlement. Private judging is voluntary and involves an adversarial procedure conducted by a retired judge whose decision may be reviewed by a public court. A variation of this last alternative is "rent-a-judge", also involving a retired judge who presides over a simplified trial, which concludes with a judgment that the parties agree by contract to respect. "Med-Arb" is a combination of traditional methods where the mediator attempts first to find an agreed solution, but if this is not successful, it automatically turns into arbitration that concludes in a final award.[88]

Hybrid procedures have also been introduced in alternative dispute resolution methods.[89] Mini-trial involves a form of structured negotiation that is not at all related to a trial or the intervention of a judge. It mainly involves the presentation of arguments by experienced lawyers to the corporate managers that are empowered to agree on a settlement, thus simplifying

---

[86] For the text of the Trust Fund Rules and Terms of Reference see (1989) 28 *International Legal Materials* 1589.

[87] Applebey, "Overview," 31.

[88] Baruch Bush, "Dispute resolution," 10–11. See also Steven J. Burton, "Combining conciliation with arbitration of international commercial disputes" 18 *Hastings International and Comparative Law Review* (1995) 637–658.

[89] Applebey, "Overview," 34.

and clarifying the issues to which the agreement relates. Summary jury trial is directed by a court and enables the parties to present their summarized arguments to a sample jury, the verdict of which is used as a basis for entering into direct negotiations. Early neutral evaluation usually involves a retired judge who hears the arguments of the parties and predicts the likely outcome of the case if brought before a court, thus facilitating the conduct of negotiations. Neutral expert fact-finding is directed to organize the facts of the case in an orderly and experienced manner, thereby also facilitating negotiations. Policy dialogue is a broader discussion of issues that do not actually represent a dispute but that do require the harmonization of different points of view.[90]

Mediation has also been combined with arbitration in various modalities. One of these is mediation followed by last or final offer arbitration, in which the arbitrator is presented with final offers from the parties who have not been able to reach agreement in the course of mediation, and is required to select between them. While on occasion mediators have followed as arbitrators in the same dispute, this should occur only exceptionally as it could affect the information received in confidence in the first stage, with implications for due process.

Some of the methods described are not unknown under international law, though they appear in a less structured manner and are more the result of practice rather than of formal definition. There are also other approaches that could be of interest for international dispute settlement as they facilitate the conduct of negotiations and the satisfactory settlement of disputes, often on an expeditious basis and consequently with reduced costs.

Apart from the interest that the methods in themselves carry, they provide important experience because of the new areas in which they are applied. Some of these new areas may be of particular relevance for international dispute settlement, in particular in the case of unusual commercial disputes. The development of small claims procedures, facilitating speedy and inexpensive justice for claims involving small amounts, could be relevant in some international transactions. Normal procedures would be far too expensive given the amount involved in the dispute and the financial capacity of the claimant.[91] Domestic experiences provide interesting insight into small claims procedures.

---

[90] For a description of these methods see Baruch Bush, "Dispute resolution," 10–11, and Applebey, "Overview," 34–36.
[91] George Applebey, "Small claims" in Samson and McBride, *Alternative Dispute Resolution*, pp. 45–51.

The recent experience of the settlement of claims relating to the Swiss dormant accounts, which involved expedited and free claims procedures, might provide some guidance on the effect of dealing with small claims generally, even though the experience failed on other grounds.[92] Interesting arrangements have also been instituted under the United Nations Compensation Commission and have also been organized with respect to slave work compensation.

The United Kingdom provides valuable experience relating to the intervention of an Insurance Ombudsman Bureau, ranging from the availability of informal advice to formal arbitration of disputes in the insurance industry, the Office of the Banking Ombudsman, the Building Societies Ombudsman Scheme and the role of the Investment Referee.[93] These are all areas where alternative dispute resolution could be usefully developed in international law as they become more and more an integral part of the global market. The extension on a global scale of financial services and transactions, for example, has not been accompanied by a dispute settlement option that might be accessible to the small investor. Globalization in these areas will very likely bring about the need for such an option.

On occasion, self-regulatory schemes of industry have provided for relevant alternatives and these are to be encouraged, although there is always the need to have dispute resolution available in case the scheme does not lead to a reasonable settlement. On the domestic level, important self-regulatory schemes such as that applicable to take-overs and mergers in the United Kingdom which involves panel decisions, particularly with a view to protect minority shareholders, are not exempt from judicial review.[94] With international take-overs and mergers being so common in a global economy, the intervention of alternative dispute settlement to protect small companies or minority shareholders might also be an important feature of the international system. This is, of course, in addition to the limited relief that might be provided under self-regulatory schemes or domestic legislation.

It should also be noted that corporations are increasingly resorting to "conflict management," including not just arbitration but a chain of settlement methods that move from negotiation to mediation and on to

---

[92] On the work and procedures of the Claims Resolution Tribunal see Thomas Buergenthal, "Arbitrating entitlement to dormant accounts" in *Liber Amicorum Ibrahim Shihata* (2000); and see further information at www.crt.ch

[93] R.W. Hodgin, "Ombudsmen and other complaints procedures in the financial services sector in the United Kingdom" in Samson and McBride, *Alternative Dispute Resolution*, pp. 168–194.

[94] Takis Tridimas, "Self-regulation and investor protection in the United Kingdom" in Samson and McBride, *Alternative Dispute Resolution*, pp. 456–487.

arbitration, each with its own features and at its own time. One important reason for this development is that ADR techniques offer the prospect to focus on the continuing interests of the parties in safeguarding their mutual relationship and not just in settling a past dispute, as may happen in arbitration. Such a continuing relationship is essential for pursuing corporate business in a global environment. Of course, arbitration will always be available as the method of last resort.

As globalization advances in the trade and financial sectors new methods for alternative dispute settlement will become increasingly desired, supplementing the role of courts or of other more established and traditional methods of dispute settlement. These developments will most likely find a source of inspiration in increasingly rich domestic experiences.

A structured international alternative dispute resolution system

The international community has at present a system of public courts, albeit limited, and also a developing alternative dispute resolution system, both likely to gather momentum in the twenty-first century. The question is whether all of the above will remain fragmented or whether it could be brought together so as to provide for an effective system of international justice. It is only natural that arrangements that form a part of the same system ought to be interrelated and not remain in isolation, as often happens as a consequence of the fragmentation of the law and dispute settlement procedures.

It must be kept in mind, however, that not all arrangements need to be integrated into some common structure, nor should there be a strict hierarchy of international tribunals or methods. This would result in curtailing the freedom of choice of the parties and the flexibility to apply specific dispute settlement in the context of particular activities or problems. It is rather a question of bringing to the parties' attention, in an organized way, the various choices at their disposal and demonstrating how these options could be properly utilized.

As has been examined above, the domestic experience provides some guidance as to the possible interrelation of courts and alternative methods. Typical cases are those of court-directed arbitration or the courts ordering the parties to pursue other options. The World Trade Organization provides an interesting example of integration under international law, combining alternative methods with panel and appellate procedures in a structure that allows to proceed from one step to another in an orderly manner.

The first step should be to encourage the referral of some cases by the International Court of Justice or other tribunals to alternative dispute resolution if this is considered useful for the settlement of the dispute. While at times of diminished judicial activity this could have conflicted with the court's own interests, this is not likely to be the case when courts work at full capacity, as is the case today and will probably be in the future. One may imagine, for example, the International Court of Justice directing the parties to undertake some form of alternative dispute resolution, before admitting a case, or at some stage in the proceedings.

In fact, both the Permanent Court[95] and the International Court of Justice have occasionally encouraged the parties to negotiate and settle in the course of the proceedings.[96] The suggestion is therefore to provide a more systematic approach and a broader scope of choices for the parties. The suggested Committee of Jurists could be of assistance in this context, as is also the case with other screening facilities that have been examined. This may prove to be an essential device if the number of judicial cases continues to increase.

The second step is to consider the development of an international supervisory function interrelating in particular arbitration with the International Court of Justice or other dispute settlement arrangements. The development of such an interrelationship is not unknown in international law. As Reisman has explained, the Permanent Court of International Justice considered itself more *par inter parem* with international arbitration, and hence did not think of becoming a supervisory institution in respect of the latter. The International Court of Justice, by contrast, has steadily moved toward envisaging for itself a broader political role that has implications in terms of the ICJ's supervisory jurisdiction that has been used in a number of cases.[97] This is likely to result in further differentiation of adjudication by way of arbitration and by the ICJ, the former emphasizing the application of the law and the latter relying on a larger political responsibility, not dissociated from the ICJ institutional role within the United Nations.[98]

---

[95] Permanent Court of International Justice, *Free Zones Case*, 1929, Ser. A. No. 24, p. 12, and discussion by Reisman, "Supervisory jurisdiction," 383.

[96] Presentation by Judge Mohamed Bedjaoui, in Connie Peck and Roy S. Lee (eds.), *Increasing the Effectiveness of the International Court of Justice* (1997), p. 23. For the guidance of the court in respect of legal issues in the *Gabcikovo-Nagymaros* case and the commitment of the parties to further negotiate on these bases, see the Report of the International Court of Justice by President Stephen M. Schwebel to the United Nations General Assembly, Fifty-second Session, 36th Plenary Meeting, 27 October 1997, Doc. A/52/PV. 36, at 2–3.

[97] Reisman, "Supervisory jurisdiction," 378.   [98] *Ibid.*, 378–379.

The practical aspects of the interrelationship between both the Permanent Court and the International Court of Justice, on the one hand, and international arbitration, on the other hand, have been examined in detail in the light of relevant cases.[99] Although the ICJ has not accepted to become a "cour de cassation *jure gentium*,"[100] still less a court of appeal, in fact it has not been far from the latter. Reisman concludes that the "*1989 Award* signals a change in the concept of its role which is a major constitutive innovation. Opposition notwithstanding, eight of the judges, six of whom were in the majority, were either espousing or engaging in what amounted to an appeal,"[101] in spite of nullity being the formal cause of action.[102] Other forms of interrelation between the ICJ and arbitration arise from the contingent appointment of arbitrators and the recognition in arbitration clauses of a legal obligation to submit to arbitration.[103]

In any event, supervision whether by way of appeal or by the right to nullify an arbitral award needs to be limited to cases involving grave violations of the law, substantial or procedural, as is the case in some arbitration arrangements that provide for nullity, for example, ICSID.[104] Otherwise instead of becoming decentralized, the system will become increasingly centralized, worsening the congestion of the courts. This is a trend already discernible under the WTO as many panel decisions have been taken to the Appellate Body. As has been suggested, the supervisory entities should develop a broad view of the role of the institution which is subject to their supervision, respecting its autonomy and its mission, if different from their own, and avoiding undue interference with its own contribution to dispute settlement.[105]

To the extent that the challenge of the validity of an international arbitral award is exceptionally allowed, it should be submitted to an independent and impartial international body, not to a domestic court that would detract from the international character of the procedures. Recent proposals include an institutionalized international review of arbitral awards: the establishment of an International Arbitral Court of Appeal,[106] and

---

[99] *Ibid.*, 340–374, with particular reference to the following cases: *Socobelge*, v. *Greece*, Permanent Court of International Justice, Ser. A/B, No. 78, (1939) 9 ILR 521; (1951) 18 ILR 3; *Arbitral Award Made by the King of Spain on 23 December 1906*, [1960] ICJ Rep. 192; and *Arbitral Award of 31 July 1989*, [1991] ICJ Rep. 53.

[100] Reisman, "Supervisory jurisdiction," 384.   [101] *Ibid.*, 342–359, at 386.

[102] *Ibid.*, 388.   [103] *Ibid.*, 382.   [104] ICSID Convention, Art. 52.

[105] Reisman, "Supervisory jurisdiction," 36–37.

[106] See generally M. Rubino-Sammartano, *International Arbitration Law* (1990).

the creation of an International Court of Arbitral Awards.[107] Judge Holtz-mann's proposal, endorsed by Judge Schwebel, former President of the International Court of Justice, is "to create a new international court that would take the place of municipal courts in resolving disputes concern-ing the enforceability of international commercial arbitration awards."[108] Standing bodies for the challenge or review of panel decisions in the context of free trade agreements have also been envisaged.

Proposals relating to supervision should, however, be approached with caution. If arbitration becomes subject to the regular supervision of courts it will become identified with ordinary court proceedings. To this extent it will become increasingly separated from other dispute settlement options and hence less of an alternative method. This is probably not the desired outcome since the interest should be in broadening the system, not in restricting it.

The above discussed interrelationship of methods is not of course restricted to courts and arbitration, but covers the whole spectrum of alter-native dispute resolution to the extent that it might be useful and conducive to a settlement. Again, as the experience of the WTO has shown, consul-tations may lead to panel decisions and these to appellate procedures, with mediation and arbitration being a possibility. "Med-Arb" is also a combi-nation of successive methods, as is conciliation followed by arbitration and many other possible connections. Last or final offer arbitration has also been discussed above.

An important role in international dispute settlement should be attributed to the principle of subsidiarity. As in a domestic context where this principle calls for state intervention only when individuals cannot appro-priately perform a social or economic function by themselves, so in interna-tional dispute settlement a privatized system of alternative dispute resolu-tion should be allowed to undertake these tasks to the fullest extent possible. Public courts should only intervene in certain types of disputes or else when exercising a supervisory function.[109]

As these various approaches are organized, guided and encouraged, the alternative dispute resolution system that has been gradually emerging will

---

[107] H. Holzmann, "A task for the 21st century: creating a new international court for resolving disputes on the enforceability of arbitral awards" in M. Hunter *et al.*, *The Internationalization of International Arbitration* (1995), pp. 109–114; S.M. Schwebel, "The creation and operation of an International Court of Arbitral Awards" in *ibid.*, pp. 115–123.

[108] Holtzmann, "Task for the 21st century," 112.

[109] For a different application of the concept of subsidiarity see supra note 35 and associated text.

become a truly global undertaking in the twenty-first century. Each method has been evolving separately towards the satisfaction of new needs and realities and additional methods are at hand. Private institutions are already providing global facilities in certain respects and it may be expected that international courts and other bodies will provide or arrange for similar functions. In this manner, the administration of broadly conceived international justice will become fully integrated with, and supplemented by, a privatized system of alternative methods,[110] which is in fact the only viable alternative for doing justice among the growing demands of the international community.

[110] Malcolm R. Wilkey, "International trade and foreign direct investment" 26 *Law and Policy in International Business* (1995) 613–631, at 615.

8

A centralized-decentralized dispute resolution system for the international community?

The basic tenet underlying the discussion in the prior chapters is that as international society moves towards centralization, at the same time it includes increasingly decentralized activities and a multiplicity of actors and subjects. Therefore, the dispute resolution system devised by such society must make available both centralized and decentralized mechanisms for attending to the social needs of this evolving structure.

As has been indicated, this dual centralized-decentralized track might appear contradictory but this is only at first sight. All societies, particularly modern ones, have developed both a central function, mostly related to the conduct of governments, and a decentralized structure, where citizens might pursue their activities with as little interference as possible from the government or the state. In fact, the most important aspect of current social evolution is how to overcome the all-encompassing and intruding role of governments that flows from the past traditions of autocratic or authoritarian rule. To the extent that this is achieved a command-free society emerges, allowing for individuals to develop their own interests and initiative, subject only to common rules of social conduct. It is in this framework that democracy has flourished as a paradigm of contemporary social arrangements.

In essence, international society is not different from modern social structures as it ultimately is concerned with providing its subjects with a better and more effective form of government. The subjects, of course, include a more varied spectrum of entities, including states and governments themselves, international organizations, individuals and corporations. Also in this context there is a need to organize social functions in the centralized-decentralized manner indicated.

Some functions ought to be centralized, such as is the case with authorization to use force, but most functions need not be subject to that approach. States have maintained a certain autonomy, but it is the need of individuals and organizations that ought to be taken into account in an international framework so that these entities may conduct business and take initiative without undue hindrance. The functions referred to as constitutional functions provide for minimum rules of social conduct in the ambit of the international community, particularly from the point of view of the interpretation and cohesiveness of the basic principles and rules of international law. Beyond that lies the immense field of freedom of action and initiative.

Establishing the limit of centralized functions is also a task for the international community so as to ensure the flourishing of democracy in its own ambit. Autocratic and authoritarian trends in international society are none too different from those known domestically and some schools of thought do indeed favor this view, consciously or unconsciously. Occasionally, these views even threaten the pursuit of democratically held values at the national level. How to achieve the right balance between what are legitimate constitutional and centralized functions in international society and what is to be preserved in the domain of decentralized activities is one of the most challenging decisions lying ahead of international law.

In their international dimension dispute settlement mechanisms must respond to the same needs. The system of public justice has been related to the work of the International Court of Justice and other, albeit limited, public tribunals, but all of them respond to a society of states, not one of individuals and other entities. This system must be enlarged to make itself available to other significant international actors and subjects of the international legal system. At the same time, the constitutional function of this system must be introduced and organized so as to allow for the orderly development of the principles and rules of international law and thus to ensure the cohesiveness of the system as a whole, including the functioning of its institutions.

A parallel system of private justice must also be fully developed and, to the extent necessary, interrelated with the public one. This alternative system is already in existence but must be perfected in its methods and coverage. This is not only so for the sake of expediency, effectiveness and cost reduction but also as an indispensable means to ensure that all relevant international actors, including those less well endowed, might have full access to dispute settlement. This objective is still far from being accomplished and to the extent that international justice does not reach all the constitutive elements of international society, it will be itself a serious obstacle for social and economic development.

More important, dispute settlement conceived in this broad dimension is a necessary guarantee for the preservation of the balanced structure of the international community and a safeguard against deviations that might affect its underlying values and principles. Checks and balances among the branches of government are also relevant in international society, above all when the nature and role of such branches are not yet well delineated, a task which essentially pertains to the courts. Safeguarding individual rights, including the very right to unimpeded access to justice, is also a judicial function relating not only to national governments but also to the very developments in international society that might be contrary to such rights. Again, it is for the courts to contribute to the orderly legal development of such society.

Beyond the elements of public policy involved in the above, there is also the very practical need to ensure that the effective functioning of world markets is further enhanced by the availability of dispute settlement mechanisms for the users of such markets. Legal certainty and predictability are today an integral part of the prospects for globalization and a condition for its success. This has become inseparable from the perfecting and development of a privatized system of international justice.

Centralized-decentralized dispute resolution arrangements, public and private mechanisms for its management, are the key equations on which the international society of the twenty-first century will be organized as far as the administration of international justice is concerned.

Bibliography

Abi-Saab, Georges, "'Humanité' et 'communauté internationale' dans la dialectique du droit international" in *Humanité et Droit International: Mélanges René-Jean Dupuy* (1991), pp. 1–2.

"De l'évolution de la cour internationale: réflexions sur quelques tendances récentes" 2 *Revue Générale de Droit International Public* (1992) 273–297.

Aboul Enein, M.I.M., "Arbitration under the auspices of the Cairo Regional Center for Commercial Arbitration" 2 *Journal of International Arbitration* (1985) 23–44.

Akande, Dapo, "The International Court of Justice and the Security Council: is there room for judicial control of decisions of the political organs of the United Nations?" 46 *International and Comparative Law Quarterly* (1997) 309–343.

Aldrich, George H., *The Jurisprudence of the Iran-United States Claims Tribunal* (1996), pp. 50–76.

Allott, Philip, *Eunomia: A New Order for a New World* (1990), pp. 135–418.

Alvarez, Henri C., "Arbitration under the North American Free Trade Agreement" 16 *Arbitration International* (2000) 393–430.

Alvarez, José E., "Judging the Security Council" 90 *American Journal of International Law* (1996) 1–39.

Amerasinghe, C.F., *The Law of the International Civil Service* (1994).

American Institute of International Law, Projects on State Responsibility, 1925 in F.V. García Amador, *The Changing Law of International Claims* (1984), vol. II, p. 826.

American Law Institute, Restatement of the Law Third, *The Foreign Relations Law of the United States* (1987), vol. 1.

Applebey, George, "An overview of alternative dispute resolution" in Claude Samson and Jeremy McBride (eds.), *Alternative Dispute Resolution* (1993), pp. 26–41.

"Small claims" in Claude Samson and Jeremy McBride (eds.), *Alternative Dispute Resolution* (1993), pp. 45–51.

Bibliography

Arangio-Ruiz, Gaetano, "The normative role of the General Assembly of the United Nations and the Declaration of Principles of Friendly Relations" *Recueil des Cours de l'Academie de Droit International* (1972, III) 624–680.

"The 'federal analogy' and UN Charter interpretation: a crucial issue" 8 *European Journal of International Law* (1997) 1–40.

Babst, Dean V., "A force for peace" 14 *Industrial Research* (1972) 55–58.

Bardonnet, Daniel (ed.), *Le Règlement Pacifique des Différends Internationaux en Europe: Perspectives d'Avenir*, Colloque de l'Académie de Droit International (1991).

Baruch Bush, Robert A., "Dispute resolution: the domestic arena – a survey of methods, applications, and critical issues" in John A. Vasquez, James Turner Johnson, Sanford Jaffe and Linda Stamato (eds.), *Beyond Confrontation: Learning Conflict Resolution in the Post-Cold War Era* (1998), pp. 9–37.

Basedow, Jürgen and Kono, Toshiyuki (eds.), *Legal Aspects of Globalization: Conflict of Laws, Internet, Capital Markets and Insolvency in a Global Economy* (2000).

Bederman, David J., comments on *The Changing Law of Nationality of Claims*, Report for the International Law Association Committee on Diplomatic Protection of Persons and Property by Francisco Orrego Vicuña, Sixty-Ninth Conference, London, 2000.

Bedjaoui, M., "Du contrôle de la légalité des actes du Conseil de Sécurité" in *Recueil d'Études en l'Honneur du Professeur François Rigaux* (1993), pp. 69–110.

Nouvel Ordre Mondial et Contrôle de la Légalité des Actes du Conseil de Sécurité (1994).

presentation in Connie Peck and Roy S. Lee (eds.), *Increasing the Effectiveness of the International Court of Justice* (1997), p. 23.

Benadava, Santiago, "La mediación de la Santa Sede en el diferendo chileno-argentino sobre la zona austral" in *International Law at a Time of Perplexity: Essays in Honour of Shabtai Rosenne* (1989), pp. 33–50.

Bilder, Richard B., "Some limitations of adjudication as an international dispute settlement technique" 23 *Virginia Journal of International Law* (1982) 1–12.

comments on *The Changing Law of Nationality of Claims*, Report for the International Law Association Committee on Diplomatic Protection of Persons and Property by Francisco Orrego Vicuña, Sixty-Ninth Conference, London, 2000.

Bissell, Richard E., "Recent practice of the Inspection Panel of the World Bank" 91 *American Journal of International Law* (1997) 741–744.

Boisson de Chazournes, Laurence, "Public participation in decision-making: the World Bank Inspection Panel" in Edith Brown Weiss, Andres Rigo Sureda and Laurence Boisson de Chazournes (eds.), *The World Bank, International Financial Institutions, and the Development of International Law*, American Society of International Law, Studies in Transnational Legal Policy, No. 31 (1999).

"Mondialisation et règlement des différends: defis et reponses" 4 *International Law Forum* (2002) 26–31.

"L'arbitrage à L'OMC" 3 *Revue de l'Arbitrage* (2003) 949–988.

Bowett, D., "The impact of Security Council decisions on dispute settlement procedures" 89 *European Journal of International Law* (1994) 5.

Boyle, Alan E., "Settlement of disputes relating to the law of the sea and the environment" in *Thesaurus Acroasium*, vol. XXVI, *International Justice* (1997), pp. 299–356.

Broches, Aron, "The Convention on the Settlement of Investment Disputes: Some Observations on Jurisdiction" 5 *Columbia Journal of International Law* (1966) 263–265.

"The Convention on the Settlement of Investment Disputes Between States and Nationals of Other States," *Recueil des Cours de l'Academie de Droit International* (1972) 355.

Brower, Charles N. and Brueschke, Jason D., *The Iran-United States Claims Tribunal* (1998), pp. 26–56.

Brown, B.S., "Primacy and complementarity: reconciling the jurisdiction of national courts and international criminal tribunals" 23 *Yale Journal of International Law* (1998) 384–436.

Brown Scott, James, *The Reports of the Hague Conferences of 1899 and 1907* (1917).

Brown Weiss, Edith, "New directions for the Great Lakes Water Quality Agreement: a commentary" 65 *Chicago-Kent Law Review* (1989) 375–386.

"The new international legal system" in *Perspectives on International Law* (1995), pp. 63–79.

"Managing international water conflicts: the Great Lakes (USA-Canada)" (unpublished paper, February 1997).

Brownlie, Ian, "International law at the fiftieth anniversary of the United Nations" 255 *Recueil des Cours de l'Academie de Droit International* (1995) 13–227.

Buergenthal, Thomas, "Arbitrating entitlement to dormant accounts" in *Liber Amicorum Ibrahim Shihata* (2000).

Bull, Hedley, "The importance of Grotius in the study of international relations" in Hedley Bull, Benedict Kingsbury and Adam Roberts (eds.), *Hugo Grotius and International Relations* (1992), pp. 65–93.

Bull, Hedley, Kingsbury, Benedict and Roberts, Adam (eds.), *Hugo Grotius and International Relations* (1992).

Burton, Steven J., "Combining conciliation with arbitration of international commercial disputes" 18 *Hastings International and Comparative Law Review* (1995) 637–658.

Caflisch, Lucius, "Vers des mécanismes pan-européens de règlement pacifique des différends" 97 *Revue Générale de Droit International Public* (1993) 1–36.

"Is the International Court of Justice entitled to review Security Council resolutions adopted under Chapter VII of the United Nations Charter?" in N. Al-Nauimi and R. Meese (eds.), *International Legal Issues Arising Under the United Nations Decade of International Law* (1995), p. 633.

Caflisch, Lucius and Cuny, Laurence, "La Cour de Conciliation et d'Arbitrage de l'OSCE: problèmes d'actualité", *OSZE Jahrbuch* (1997) 4.

Cameron, James and Campbell, Karen, *Dispute Resolution in the World Trade Organisation* (1998).

Bibliography

Cameron, James and Gray, Kevin R., "Principles of international law in the WTO Dispute Settlement Body" 50 *International and Comparative Law Quarterly* (2001) 248–298.

Cardona Llorens, Jorge, "La coopération entre les Nations Unies et les accords et organismes régionaux pour le réglément pacifique des affaires relatives au maintien de la paix et de la sécurité internationales" in *Boutros Boutros-Ghali Amicorum Discipulorumque Liber* (1998), pp. 251–289.

Caron, David D., "The nature of the Iran-United States Claims Tribunal and the evolving structure of international dispute resolution" 84 *American Journal of International Law* (1990) 104–156.

Cassese, Antonio, "Les individus" in Mohammed Bedjaoui (rédacteur général), *Droit International: Bilan et Persectives* (1991), pp. 119–127.

Cerar, B., comments on *The Changing Law of Nationality of Claims*, Report for the International Law Association Committee on Diplomatic Protection of Persons and Property by Francisco Orrego Vicuña, Sixty-Ninth Conference, London, 2000.

Charney, Jonathan, "Third party dispute settlement and international law" 36 *Columbia Journal of Transnational Law* (1997) 65–89.

Charnovitz, Steve, "The WTO and the rights of the individual" 36 *Intereconomics* (2001) 98–108.

Cherif Bassiouni, M., "Policy perspectives favoring the establishment of the International Criminal Court" 52 *Journal of International Affairs* (1999) 795–810.

Chinkin, C.M., "The challenge of soft law: development and change in international law" 38 *International and Comparative Law Quarterly* (1989) 850–866.

"Increasing the use and appeal of the Court" in Connie Peck and Roy S. Lee (eds.), *Increasing the Effectiveness of the International Court of Justice* (1997), pp. 50–56.

Coombe, George W., "The future: implementing new approaches to the settlement of transnational commercial disputes" 17 *Canada-United States Law Journal* (1991) 533–590.

Covelli, Nick, "Public international law and third party participation in WTO Panel Proceedings" 33 *Journal of World Trade* (1999) 125–140.

Crawford, James, "Democracy and international law," *British Year Book of International Law* (1993) 123.

"The Charter of the United Nations as a Constitution" in Hazel Fox (ed.), *The Changing Constitution of the United Nations* (1997), pp. 3–16.

Croley, Steven P. and Jackson, John H., "WTO dispute procedures: standard of review, and deference to national governments" 90 *American Journal of International Law* (1996) 193.

Cuny, Laurence, *L'OSCE et le Règlement Pacifique des Différends: La Cour de Conciliation et d'Arbitrage* (IHEI 1997) 68–69.

Da Cruz Vilaça, José Luis, "La protection des droits des particuliers et le systéme juridictionnel communautaire dans le Traité d'Amsterdam" in Juan Manuel

Bibliography

de Faramiñán Gilbert (Co-ordinator), *Reflexiones en Torno al Tratado de Amsterdam y el Futuro de la Unión Europea* (2000), pp. 245–271.

Del Vecchio, Angela, *Aspetti dell' Integrazione Regionale Latinoamericana* (2001).

Giurisdizione Internazionale e Globalizzazione (2003).

Denza, Eileen, "Two legal orders: divergent or convergent?" 48 *International and Comparative Law Quarterly* (1999) 257–284.

Dolzer, Rudolf, "Diplomatic protection of foreign nationals" in *Encyclopedia of Public International Law* (1992), pp. 1067–1070.

Dupuy, Pierre-Marie, "The constitutional dimension of the Charter of the United Nations revisited" 1 *Max Planck Yearbook of United Nations Law* (1997) 1–33.

"The danger of fragmentation or unification of the international legal system and the International Court of Justice" 31 *New York University Journal of International Law and Politics* (1999) 791–807.

Durante, Francesco, *Ricorsi Individuali ad Organi Internazionali: Contributo alla Teoria della Personalità Internazionale dell'Individuo* (1958).

Encyclopedia of Public International Law (1992), pp. 1050–1056.

Endsley, Harry B., "Dispute settlement under the CFTA and NAFTA: from eleventh-hour innovation to accepted institution" 18 *Hastings International and Comparative Law Review* (1995) 659–711.

Fassbender, Bardo, *The UN Security Council Reform and the Right of Veto: A Constitutional Perspective* (1997).

"The United Nations Charter as Constitution of the international community" 36 *Columbia Journal of Transnational Law* (1998) 529–619.

Feliciano, Florentino P., "Dispute settlement under the aegis of the World Trade Organization" in Antonio M. Elicaño, *Odyssey and Legacy: The Chief Justice Andrés R. Narvasa Centennial Lecture Series* (1998), pp. 179–202, lecture delivered on 12 November 1998, at 192–197.

Feliciano, Florentino P. and Van den Bossche, Peter L.H., "The dispute settlement system of the World Trade Organization: institutions, process and practice" 75 *Philippine Law Journal* (2000) 1–46.

Fernandez, C.C. and Spolter, J., "International intellectual property dispute resolution: is mediation a sleeping giant?" 53 *Dispute Resolution Journal* (1998) 62–69.

Foundation for International Environmental Law and Development (FIELD) and Center on International Co-operation, New York University, meeting on *Funding of and Access to International Courts and Dispute Settlement Bodies*, report, London, 31 January–1 February 1997.

Fox, Lady H., comments on *The Changing Law of Nationality of Claims*, Report for the International Law Association Committee on Diplomatic Protection of Persons and Property by Francisco Orrego Vicuña, Sixty-Ninth Conference, London, 2000.

Friedmann, Wolfgang, *The Changing Structure of International Law* (1964).

Bibliography

Frigessi di Rattalma, Marci, "Le régime de responsabilité internationale institué par le Conseil d'Administration de la Commission de Compensation des Nations Unies" 101 *Revue Générale de Droit International Public* (1997) 45.

Fukuyama, Francis, "The end of history?" 16 *The National Interest* (Summer 1989) 3–18.

García Amador, F.V., *The Inter-American System* (1983).

The Changing Law of International Claims (1984), vol. II.

Revised Draft on State Responsibility prepared for the International Law Commission, 1961, in F.V. García Amador, *The Changing Law of International Claims* (1984), vol. II, pp. 504–795.

García-Valdecasas, Rafael, "El Tribunal de Primera Instancia de las Comunidades Europeas" in Gil Carlos Rodriguez Iglesias and Diego J. Liñan Nogueras (eds.), *El Derecho Comunitario Europeo y su Aplicación Judicial* (1995), p. 403.

Geck, Wilhelm Karly, "Diplomatic protection" in *Encyclopedia of Public International Law* (1992), pp. 1046–1056.

Goldberg, Green and Sander, *Dispute Resolution* (1985).

Gray, Christine and Kingsbury, Benedict, "Developments in dispute settlement: inter-state arbitration since 1945," *British Year Book of International Law* (1992) 97–134.

Guillaume, Gilbert, "The future of international judicial institutions" 44 *International and Comparative Law Quarterly* (1995) 848.

Hambro, Edward I., "Individuals before international tribunals," *Proceedings of the American Society of International Law* (1941) 22–29.

Hauriou, M., "La théorie de l'institution et de la fondation: essai de vitalisme social" in *La Cité Moderne et les Transformations du Droit*, 4 *Cahiers de la Nouvelle Journée* (1925) 1–11.

Hefferman, Liz, "The Community courts post-Nice: a European *certiorari* revisited" 52 *ICLQ* (2003) 907–933.

Heiskanen, Veijo and O'Brien, Robert, "UN Compensation Commission Panel sets precedents on government claims" 92 *American Journal of International Law* (1998) 339–350.

Held, David (ed.), *A Globalizing World?: Culture, Economics, Politics* (2000).

Held, David and McGrew, Anthony, *Globalization and Anti-Globalization* (2002).

Hey, Ellen, *Reflections on an International Environmental Court* (2000).

Higgins, Rosalyn, "Conceptual thinking about the individual in international law" in Falk, Kratochwil and Mendlovitz (eds.), *International Law: A Contemporary Perspective* (1985), pp. 476–494.

"International law in a changing international system" 58 *Cambridge Law Journal* (1999) 78–95.

Hippler Bello, Judith, "The WTO Dispute Settlement Understanding: less is more" 90 *American Journal of International Law* (1996) 416–417.

Hodgin, R.W., "Ombudsmen and other complaints procedures in the financial services sector in the United Kingdom" in Claude Samson and Jeremy McBride (eds.), *Alternative Dispute Resolution* (1993), pp. 168–194.

Holtzmann, Howard M., *A Guide to the UNCITRAL Model Law on International Commercial Arbitration: Legislative History and Commentary* (1988).

"Dispute resolution in Europe under the UNCITRAL Conciliation Rules" in Daniel Bardonnet (ed.), *Le Règlement Pacifique des Différends Internationaux en Europe: Perspectives d'Avenir*, Colloque de l'Académie de Droit International (1991), pp. 293–303.

"A task for the 21st century: creating a new international court for resolving disputes on the enforceability of arbitral awards" in M. Hunter *et al.*, *The Internationalization of International Arbitration* (1995), pp. 109–114.

Hudec, M.E., *Enforcing International Trade Law: The Evolution of the Modern GATT Legal System* (1993).

Hunter, Martin, "International commercial dispute resolution: the challenge of the twenty-first century" 16 *Arbitration International* (2000) 379–392.

Institut de Droit International, "Resolution on the national character of an international claim presented by a state for injury suffered by an individual," 10 September 1965, 51-II *Annuaire* (1965) 260.

Instituto de Investigaciones Jurídicas, Universidad Nacional Autonoma de México, *Resolución de Controversias Comerciales en América del Norte* (1997).

International Bureau of the Permanent Court of Arbitration, *International Alternative Dispute Resolution: Past, Present and Future* (2000).

Jackson, John H., "The WTO Dispute Settlement Understanding: misunderstandings on the nature of legal obligations" 91 *American Journal of International Law* (1997) 60.

The World Trade Organization: Constitution and Jurisprudence (1998), pp. 48–97.

The Jurisprudence of GATT and the WTO (2000).

Jenks, C.W., *The Common Law of Mankind* (1958), p. 23.

Jennings, Robert Y., "The role of the International Court of Justice" 68 *British Year Book of International Law* (1997) 1–63.

Jennings, Robert and Watts, Arthur, *Oppenheim's International Law* (1992), vol. 1.

Joliet, R. and Vogel, W., "Le Tribunal de Premiere Instance des Communautés Européennes" 329 *Revue du Marché Commun* (1989) 424.

Kennedy, Paul, *The Rise and Fall of Great Powers* (1987).

Killmann, Bernd-Roland, "The access of individuals to international trade dispute settlement" 13 *Journal of International Arbitration* (1996) 143–169.

Koh, Pearlie M.C., "Enhancing economic co-operation: a regional arbitration centre for ASEAN?" 49 *International and Comparative Law Quarterly* (2000) 390–412.

Kokott, J., comments on *The Changing Law of Nationality of Claims*, Report for the International Law Association Committee on Diplomatic Protection of

Persons and Property by Francisco Orrego Vicuña, Sixty-Ninth Conference, London, 2000.

Kriesberg, Louis, "Applications and misapplications of conflict resolution ideas to international conflicts" in John A. Vasquez, James Turner Johnson, Sanford Jaffe and Linda Stamato (eds.), *Beyond Confrontation: Learning Conflict Resolution in the Post-Cold War Era* (1998), pp. 87–102.

Lacarte-Muró, Julio, "Developing countries and the WTO legal and dispute settlement system: a view from the bench", speech delivered to the UNCTAD Workshop on Settlement of Disputes in International Trade, Investment and Intellectual Property, Geneva, 20–22 January 2000.

Lauterpacht, Elihu, "The World Bank Convention on the Settlement of International Investment Disputes," *Recueil d'Études de Droit International en Hommage à Paul Guggenheim* (1968) 642–664.

Lauterpacht, Hersch, *The Function of Law in the International Community* (1933). *International Law and Human Rights* (1950).

Lee, Roy S., comments on Francisco Orrego Vicuña and Christopher Pinto, *The Peaceful Settlement of Disputes: Prospects for the Twenty-first Century*, Final Report for the Centennial Commemoration of the First Peace Conference, May 1999, published in F. Kalhoven (ed.), *The Centennial of the First Peace Conference* (2000).

Lillich, Richard B. (ed.), *The United Nations Compensation Commission* (1995).

Lillich, Richard B. and Weston, Burns H., *International Claims: Their Settlement by Lump Sum Agreements* (1975).

Lillich, Richard B. and Magraw, Daniel B. (eds.), *The Iran-United States Claims Tribunal: Its Contribution to the Law of State Responsibility* (1998).

Lowe, Vaughan, comments on *The Changing Law of Nationality of Claims*, Report for the International Law Association Committee on Diplomatic Protection of Persons and Property by Francisco Orrego Vicuña, Sixty-Ninth Conference, London, 2000.

Macdonald, R.St.J., "The United Nations Charter: constitution or contract?" in R.St.J. Macdonald and Douglas M. Johnston (eds.), *The Structure and Process of International Law* (1983), pp. 889–912.

"The Charter of the United Nations and the development of fundamental principles of international law" in Bin Cheng and E.D. Brown (eds.), *Contemporary Problems of International Law* (1988), pp. 196–215.

Martínez Puñal, Antonio, *La Solución de Controversias en el Mercado Común del Sur (MERCOSUR): Estudio de sus Mecanismos* (2000).

McDougal, Myres S. *et al.*, "The world constitutive process of authoritative decision" in Myres S. McDougal and W. Michael Reisman, *International Law Essays: A Supplement to International Law in Contemporary Perspective* (1981), pp. 191–192.

McWhinney, Edward, "The International Court as a Constitutional Court and the blurring of the arbitral/judicial processes" 6 *Leiden Journal of International Law* (1993) 279–295.

Bibliography

Menon, P.K., "The subjects of modern international law" 3 *Hague Yearbook of International Law* (1990) 30–86.

Mensah, Thomas A., "The dispute settlement regime of the 1982 United Nations Convention on the Law of the Sea" 2 *Max Planck Yearbook of United Nations Law* (1998) 307–323.

"The role of peaceful dispute settlement in contemporary ocean policy" in Davor Vidas and Willy Ostreng, *Order for the Oceans at the Turn of the Century* (1999), pp. 81–94.

Merrills, J.G., *International Dispute Settlement* (1998).

Mestre, A., "Les traités et le droit interne" 42 *Recueil des Cours de l'Academie de Droit International* (1931, IV) 233–301.

Moitinho de Almeida, José Carlos, "Evolución jurisprudencial en materia de acceso de los particulares a la jurisdicción comunitaria" in Gil Carlos Rodriguez Iglesias and Diego J. Liñan Nogueras (eds.), *El Derecho Comunitario Europeo y su Aplicación Judicial* (1995), pp. 595–630.

Mosler, Hermann, "The international society as a legal community" *Recueil des Cours de l'Academie de Droit International* (1974, IV) 1–320.

Mueller, John, *Retreat from Doomsday: The Obsolescence of Major War* (1989).

Neville Brown, L., "Alternative dispute resolution tribunals" in Claude Samson and Jeremy McBride (eds.), *Alternative Dispute Resolution* (1993), pp. 84–95.

Nørgaard, C., *The Position of the Individual in International Law* (1962).

Oda, Shigeru, "The compulsory jurisdiction of the International Court of Justice: a myth?" 49 *International and Comparative Law Quarterly* (2000) 251–277.

Ohly, D.C., "A functional analysis of claimant eligibility" in R.B. Lillich (ed.), *International Law of State Responsibility for Injuries to Aliens* (1983), pp. 281–291.

Onuf, Nicholas, "The Constitution of international society" 5 *European Journal of International Law* (1994), 5, s. III.

Orrego Vicuña, Francisco, "Report on Chile" in Elihu Lauterpacht and John G. Collier, *Individual Rights and the State in Foreign Affairs* (1977), pp. 123–186.

"The settlement of disputes and conflict resolution in the context of a re-vitalized role for the United Nations Security Council" in R.-J. Dupuy (ed.), *The Development of the Role of the Security Council* (1993), p. 41.

The Changing Law of Nationality of Claims, Report for the International Law Association Committee on Diplomatic Protection of Persons and Property, Sixty-Ninth Conference, London, 2000.

"The review of managerial discretion by international administrative tribunals: comments in the light of the practice of the World Bank Administrative Tribunal," paper presented at the Conference on the Commemoration of the Twentieth Anniversary of the World Bank Administrative Tribunal, Paris, 16 May 2000.

Orrego Vicuña, Francisco, and Pinto, Christopher, *The Peaceful Settlement of Disputes: Prospects for the Twenty-first Century*, Final Report for the Centennial

135

Bibliography

Commemoration of the First Peace Conference, May 1999, published in F. Kalhoven (ed.), *The Centennial of the First Peace Conference* (2000), p. 388.

Palmer, Geoffrey, "New ways to make international environmental law" 86 *American Journal of International Law* (1992) 259–283.

Palmeter, David and Mavroidis, Petros C., *Dispute Settlement in the World Trade Organization* (1999).

Pan, Eric J., "Assessing the NAFTA Chapter 19 binational panel system: an experiment in international adjudication" 40 *Harvard International Law Journal* (1999) 379–449.

Parra, Antonio R., "Provisions on the settlement of investment disputes in modern investment laws, Bilateral Investment Treaties and multilateral instruments on investment" 12 *ICSID Review-Foreign Investment Law Journal* (1997) 287–364.

Paulsson, Jan, "Arbitration without privity" 10 *ICSID Review Foreign Investment Law Journal* (1995) 232.

"Fast-track arbitration in Europe (with special reference to the WIPO Expedited Arbitration Rules)" 18 *Hastings International and Comparative Law Review* (1995) 713–717.

Pearlman, Jessica C., "Participation by private counsel in World Trade Organization dispute settlement proceedings" 30 *Law and Policy in International Business* (1999) 399–416.

Peck, Connie, and Lee, Roy S. (eds.), *Increasing the Effectiveness of the International Court of Justice* (1997).

Petersmann, Ernst-Ulrich, "The dispute settlement system of the World Trade Organization and the evolution of the GATT dispute settlement system since 1948" 31 *Common Market Law Review* (1994) 1157–1244.

The GATT/WTO Dispute Settlement System: International Law, International Organizations and Dispute Settlement (1996).

"Alternative dispute settlement in international trade, investment and intellectual property law: an overview," UNCTAD Workshop on Settlement of Disputes in International Trade, Investment and Intellectual Property, 20–22 January 2000, 23.

Pinto, M.C.W., "Structure, process, outcome: thoughts on the 'essence' of international arbitration" 6 *Leiden Journal of International Law* (1993) 241–264.

"The Court and other international tribunals" in Connie Peck and Roy S. Lee (eds.), *Increasing the Effectiveness of the International Court of Justice* (1997), pp. 281–309.

Poulantzas, Nicholas, "The individual before international jurisdiction" 15 *Revue Héllenique de Droit International* (1962) 375–390.

Reisman, W. Michael, "The constitutional crisis in the United Nations" 87 *American Journal of International Law* (1993) 83.

"The supervisory jurisdiction of the International Court of Justice: international arbitration and international adjudication" 258 *Recueil des Cours de l'Academie de Droit International* (1996) 9–394.

Renard, G., "Les bases philosophiques du droit international et la doctrine du 'Bien commun,'" *Archives de Philosophie du Droit* (1931) 465–477.

Rest, Alfred, "The indispensability of an international environmental court" 7 *Review of European Community and International Environmental Law* (1998) 63–67.

Rey Caro, Ernesto J., *La Solución de Controversias en los Procesos de Integración en América: El Mercosur* (1998), pp. 22–111.

El Protocolo de Olivos para la Solucion de Controversias en el MERCOSUR (2002).

Reymond, Christophe, "Institutions, decision-making procedure and settlement of disputes in the European Economic Area" 30 *Common Market Law Review* (1993) 449–480.

Rodriguez Iglesias, Carlos, Gil and Liñan Nogueras, Diego J. (eds.), *El Derecho Comunitario Europeo y su Aplicación Judicial* (1995).

Rosenne, Shabtai, "Reflections on the position of the individual in inter-state litigation in the International Court of Justice" in *International Arbitration, Liber Amicorum for Martin Domke* (1967), pp. 113–240.

reply, 29 *Virginia Journal of International Law* (1989) 401.

An International Law Miscellany (1993).

The Law and Practice of the International Court, 1920–1996 (1997).

"Lessons of the past and needs of the future" in Connie Peck and Roy S. Lee (eds.), *Increasing the Effectiveness of the International Court of Justice* (1997), pp. 466–492.

Rostow, W.W., "The coming age of regionalism: a 'metaphor' for our time?," *Encounter* (June 1990) 3–7.

Rubin, Alfred P., "Challenging the conventional wisdom: another view of the International Criminal Court" 52 *Journal of International Affairs* (1999) 783–794.

Rubino-Sammartano, M., *International Arbitration Law* (1990).

Ruiz Fabri, Hélène, "L'appel dans le règlement des différends de l'OMC: trois ans après, quinze rapports plus tard" 103 *Revue Générale de Droit International Public* (1999) 47–128.

Rummel, R.J., "Libertarianism and international violence" 27 *Journal of Conflict Resolution* (1983) 27–71.

Russett, Bruce, "The politics of an alternative security system: toward a more democratic and therefore more peaceful world" in Burns Weston (ed.), *Alternatives to Nuclear Deterrence* (1989).

St. Korowicz, Marek, "The problem of the international personality of individuals" 50 *American Journal of International Law* (1956) 533–562.

Scelle, G., "Droit de la paix" 46 *Recueil des Cours de l'Academie de Droit International* (1933, IV) 660–661.

"Le droit constitutionnel international" in *Mélanges R. Carré de Malberg* (1933), pp. 503–515.

Précis de Droit des Gens, Tome II (1934), pp. 410–411.

Schachter, Oscar, *International Law in Theory and Practice* (1991), p. 10.

Bibliography

Schermers, Henry and Waelbroeck, Denis, *Judicial Protection in the European Communities* (1987).

Schlemmer-Schulte, Sabine, "Introductory note to the conclusions of the second review of the World Bank Inspection Panel" (2000) 39 *International Legal Materials* 243.

Schleyer, Glen T., "Power to the people: allowing private parties to raise claims before the WTO dispute resolution system," *Fordham Law Review* (1997) 2275.

Schloemann, Hannes L. and Ohlhoff, Stefan, "'Constitutionalization' and dispute settlement in the WTO: national security as an issue of competence" 93 *American Journal of International Law* (1999) 424–451.

Schneider, Michael E., "How fair and efficient is the United Nations Compensation Commission system?" 15 *Journal of International Arbitration* (1998) 15–26.

Schoenbaum, Thomas J., "WTO dispute settlement: praise and suggestions for reform" 47 *International and Comparative Law Quarterly* (1998) 647–658.

Schreuer, C., "Commentary on the ICSID Convention: Article 25" 11 *ICSID Review-Foreign Investment Law Journal* (1996) 318–391.

The ICSID Convention: A Commentary (2001).

Schwarzenberger, G., *International Law as Applied by International Courts and Tribunals* (1957).

"International law as applied by international courts and tribunals" in *International Constitutional Law* (1976) vol. III, pp. 116–117.

Schwebel, Stephen M., *International Arbitration: Three Salient Problems* (1987).

"Preliminary rulings by the International Court of Justice at the instance of national courts" 28 *Virginia Journal of International Law* (1988) 495.

"The creation and operation of an International Court of Arbitral Awards" in M. Hunter *et al.*, *The Internationalization of International Arbitration* (1995), pp. 115–123.

"Fifty years of the World Court: a critical appraisal," *Proceedings of the American Society of International Law* (1996), pp. 339–347.

Scott, James Brown, *The Reports of the Hague Conferences of 1899 and 1907* (1917).

Shihata, Ibrahim F.I., "Implementation, enforcement and compliance with international environmental agreements: practical suggestions in light of the World Bank's experience" 9 *Georgetown International Environmental Law Review* (1996) 37–51.

Complementary Reform (1997).

Complementary Reform: Essays on Legal, Judicial and Other Institutional Reforms Supported by the World Bank (1998).

"The World Bank Inspection Panel: its historical, legal and operational aspects" in *The World Bank in a Changing World* (2000), pp. 537–601.

The World Bank Inspection Panel (2000).

Shihata, Ibrahim F.I. and Parra, Antonio R., "The experience of the International Centre for Settlement of Investment Disputes" 14 *ICSID Review-Foreign Investment Law Journal* (1999) 299–361.

Skubiszewski, K., "The ICJ and the Security Council" in *Fifty Years of the International Court of Justice: Essays in Honour of Sir Robert Jennings* (1996), p. 616.

Sluiter, G., "An International Criminal Court is hereby established" 16 *Netherlands Quarterly of Human Rights* (1998) 413–420.

Societé Française pour le Droit International, *L'État Souverain à l'Aube du XXIe Siècle*, Colloque de Nancy (1994).

Sohn, Louis B., "Draft General Treaty on the Peaceful Settlement of International Disputes: a proposal and report," American Bar Association, Committee on World Order Under Law, 20 *The International Lawyer* (1986) 261–291.

"The role of international law in the 21st century," address made at Vrije Universiteit, Brussels, 23 March 1990, 5–6.

"The Use of Consultations for Monitoring Compliance with Agreements Concluded under the Auspices of International Organizations (1993), pp. 80–284.

"Bipartite Consultative Commissions for preventing and resolving disputes relating to international trade treaties" in *International Law in an Evolving World*, *Liber Amicorum Eduardo Jiménez de Aréchaga* (1994), pp. 1181–1200.

"Broadening the Role of the United Nations in Preventing, Mitigating or Ending International or Internal Conflicts that Threaten International Peace and Security," International Rule of Law Center Occasional Papers, Second Series, No. 1 (1997).

comments, in Connie Peck and Roy S. Lee (eds.), *Increasing the Effectiveness of the International Court of Justice* (1997), p. 67.

Sohn, Louis B. and Baxter, Richard R., Draft Convention on International Responsibility prepared for the Harvard Law School, 1961, in García Amador, *The Changing Law of International Claims* (1984), vol. II, p. 858.

Specht, Patrick, "The dispute settlement systems of WTO and NAFTA: analysis and comparison" 27 *Georgia Journal of International and Comparative Law* (1998) 57–138.

Sullivan, Daniel S., "Effective international dispute settlement mechanisms and the necessary condition of liberal democracy" 81 *Georgetown Law Journal* (1993) 2369–2412.

Suy, Eric, "The constitutional character of constituent Treaties of international organizations and the hierarchy of norms" in *Recht Zwischen Umbruch und Bewahrung*, *Festschrift für Rudolf Bernhardt* (1995), pp. 125, 267–277.

"Symposium on the first three years of the WTO dispute settlement system" 32 *The International Lawyer* (1998) 609.

Symposium on the International Criminal Court, "A Critical Review of the Results of the Rome Conference," convened in honor of Judge Antonio Cassese, Erasmus University, Rotterdam, 5 November 1998.

"The triumph of nations," *The Economist: The World in 2001* (2001) 42–43.

Tomuschat, Christian, "Obligations arising for states without or against their will" 241 *Recueil des Cours de l'Academie de Droit International* (1993, IV) 195–292.

"International law as the constitution of mankind" in *United Nations: International Law on the Eve of the Twenty-first Century* (1997), pp. 37–50.

Bibliography

Torres Bernárdez, Santiago, "L'arbitrage interétatique" in Daniel Bardonnet (ed.), *Le Règlement Pacifique des Différends Internationaux en Europe: Perspectives d'Avenir*, Colloque de l'Académie de Droit International (1991), pp. 205–267.

Trakman, Leon E., *Dispute Settlement under the NAFTA* (1997).

Trevor-Roper Hugh and Urban, George, "Aftermaths of Empire: the lessons of upheavals and destabilisation," *Encounter* (December 1989) 3–16.

Tridimas, Takis, "Self-regulation and investor protection in the United Kingdom" in Claude Samson and Jeremy McBride (eds.), *Alternative Dispute Resolution* (1993), pp. 456–487.

Urquhart, Brian, *The United Nations: From Peace-Keeping to a Collective System?* (1991).

Valticos, Nicolas, "Checks exerted by administrative tribunals over the discretionary powers of international organizations," paper presented at the Conference on the Commemoration of the Twentieth Anniversary of the World Bank Administrative Tribunal, Paris, 16 May 2000.

Van der Borght, Kim, review of David Palmeter and Petros C. Mavroidis, *Dispute Settlement in the World Trade Organization* (1999) 94 *American Journal of International Law* (2000) 427–430.

Vanduzer, J. Anthony, "Investor-state dispute settlement under NAFTA Chapter 11: the shape of things to come?" 35 *Canadian Yearbook of International Law* (1997) 263–290.

Vasquez, John A., "The learning of peace: lessons from a multidisciplinary inquiry" in John A. Vasquez, James Turner Johnson, Sanford Jaffe and Linda Stamato (eds.), *Beyond Confrontation: Learning Conflict Resolution in the Post-Cold War Era* (1998), pp. 211–238.

Vasquez, John A., Turner Johnson, James, Jaffe, Sanford and Stamato, Linda (eds.), *Beyond Confrontation: Learning Conflict Resolution in the Post-Cold War Era* (1998).

Verdross, A., *Die Verfassung der Völkerrechtsgemeinschaft* (1926).
Völkerrecht (2nd edn., 1950; 5th edn., 1964).

Verdross, A. and Simma, Bruno, *Universelles Völkerrecht: Theorie und Praxis* (1976), p. 5.

Vermulst, Edwin, Mavroidis, Petros C. and Waer, Paul, "The functioning of the Appellate Body after four years: towards rule integrity" 33 *Journal of World Trade* (1999) 1–50.

Von der Heydte, F., "L'individu et les tribunaux internationaux" *Recueil des Cours de l'Academie de Droit International* (1962, III) 287–358.

Waelbroeck, M., Louis, J.V. and Vandersanden, G., "Le droit de la Communauté Economique Européenne" in *La Cour de Justice, Les actes des Institutions* (1983), vol. 10.

Wälde, T., "Investment arbitration under the Energy Charter Treaty: from dispute settlement to Treaty implementation" 12 *Arbitration International* (1996) 429.

Wang, Margaret, "Are alternative dispute resolution methods superior to litigation in resolving disputes in international commerce?" 16 *Arbitration International* (2000) 189–211.

Warbrick, C., "Protection of nationals abroad: current legal problems" 37 *International and Comparative Law Quarterly* (1988) 1003, 1006.

Weil, Prosper, "Le droit international en quéte de son identité," Cours Général de Droit International Public 237 *Recueil des Cours de l'Académie de Droit International* (1992, VI) 13–369.

Weinstein, J.B., "Some benefits and risks of privatization of justice through ADR" 11 *Ohio State Journal on Dispute Resolution* (1996) 241.

Weiss, Friedl (ed.), *Improving WTO Dispute Settlement Procedures* (2000).

Weller, M., "The reality of the emerging universal constitutional order" X *Cambridge Review of International Affairs* (1997) 41.

Weston, Burns H., Lillich, Richard B. and Bederman, David J., *International Claims: Their Settlement by Lump Sum Agreements: 1975–1995* (1999).

Wilkey, Malcolm R., "International trade and foreign direct investment" 26 *Law and Policy in International Business* (1995) 613–631.

Woodman, Gordon R., "The alternative law of alternative dispute resolution" in Claude Samson and Jeremy McBride (eds.), *Alternative Dispute Resolution* (1993), pp. 580–605.

World Bank Guidelines on the Treatment of Foreign Direct Investment 7 *ICSID Review-Foreign Investment Law Journal* (1992) 295.

Ziadé, Nassib G., "Some practical issues arising in international administrative tribunals," paper presented at Conference on the Commemoration of the Twentieth Anniversary of the World Bank Administrative Tribunal, Paris, 16 May 2000.

Index

Index

arbitration (*cont.*)
  ITLOS and 81–82
  NAFTA and 68–69
  private arbitration 113–115
  subsidiarity and 122
  WTO and 87
ASEAN Agreement for the Promotion and
  Protection of Investments (1987) 68

Babst, J. 3
Baruch Bush, R.A. 99, 116–117
Basedow, J. and Kono, T. 3–4
Bassiouni, M.C. 55–56
Beagle Channel (Papal Mediation 1980) 107
Bederman, D.J. 32–33
Bedjaoui, M. 23–24, 120
Bello, J.H. 89
Benadava, S. 107
Bennouna, M. 31–32
Bilder, R.B. 99–100
Bissell, R.E. 79–80
BITs (bilateral investment treaties)
  MFN clauses, extension to dispute settlement
    provisions 67
  proliferation 66
Boisson de Chazournes, L. 79, 80
Bowett, D. 23–24
Boyle, A.E. 81–82
Broches, A. 65, 66
Brower, C.N. and Brueschke, J.D. 42–44
Brown, B.S. 55–56
Brown Weiss, E. 2, 6, 7–8
Brownlie, I. 12
Buergenthal, T. 117–118
Bull, Hedley 1

Caflisch, L. 23–24
Caflisch, L. and Cluny, L. 105–106
Cameron, J. and Campbell, K. 86
Campbell, J. and Gray, K.R. 91
Canada–US Free Trade Agreement 1988 71,
  103–104
Caron, D.D. 42–43
Cassese, A. 52
Center for Public Resources Institute for Dispute
  Resolution 114
Central American Court of Justice (1907–18)
  49
Central American Court of Justice (1992–): *see
  also* Andean Court of Justice
  as administrative tribunal 77

consent, relevance 77
as constitutional court
  in disputes between state organs 77
  treaty interpretation and 77
individual, standing, non-compliance with
  judicial decisions 77
Charney, J.I. 18
Chile
  diplomatic protection 33
  Truth and Reconciliation Commission 106
Chile–US Commission for the Settlement of
  Disputes 106
Chinkin, C.M. 5, 21, 22
collective security 2
Commercial Arbitration and Mediation Center
  of the Americas 113–114
compliance 52
  alternative dispute settlement procedures and
    104, 111
  enforcement mechanism, relevance 64, 111
  WTO 87–88, 90
conciliation
  compulsory recourse to 106
    Chile–Argentina, Treaty of Peace and
     Friendship (1984) 106
  Convention on Conciliation and Arbitration
    in the Framework of the OSCE (1992)
    105
  subsidiarity and 105–106
  good offices and 105–106
  popularity 105
confidentiality/transparency
  mediation 107
  NAFTA 95–96
  WTO Dispute Settlement Understanding
    (DSU) 95
conflict management 118–119
constitutional court, proposals for (Centennial
  Commemoration of First Peace
  Conference): *see also* International Court
  of Justice as constitutional court; Security
  Council, Judicial review
  composition 28
  consent of states, relevance 27–28
  constitution, relevance 27
  constitutional structure, relevance 27
  equality of states and 27–28
  jurisdiction 28
  recommendation for further study 27
  separation of powers, relevance 27
  sovereignty and 27

144

Index

145

Index

Index

Index

NAFTA (*cont.*)
  recognition and enforcement of awards 72–73
national autonomy, need to preserve 8–9
national courts: *see* domestic courts
nationalism 4
nationality of claims 31–47: *see also* diplomatic protection; individual, standing before international tribunal; Iran–US Claims Tribunal; lump sum claims settlement agreements; nationality of corporation
  continuity of nationality 32, 36–37, 46–47
    advantages of rule 36–37
    critical date considerations 37
    Helms-Burton Act 1996 37
    inconsistency with state's espousal of claim doctrine 32, 36
    state practice 36
  double nationality
    changing practice 46–47
    dominant and effective nationality 39–40
    Hague Convention on the Conflict of Nationality Laws (1930) 39
    Iran–US Claims Tribunal practice 39–40, 43
    joint action, possibility of 39–40
    Mergé 39, 43
    military service and 35–36
  ECJ and 74–75
  espousal of claim of national of defendant state 34–35
  exceptions to rule 34–36
    declaration of intention to acquire nationality of espousing state 34
    distribution of compensation to non-nationals 34
    espousal of claim of non-national 35–36: in domestic courts 35–36; European Union practice 35–36
    European Union practice of consular and diplomatic assistance 34
    human rights 53
    OECD policy 35–36
    Reparations for Injuries case 34
    UN Compensation Commission practice 44–45
  genuine and effective link (*Nottebohm*) 33–34, 43
  ICSID: *see* ICSID, "national of another contracting state"
  ITLOS 82

married women 35–36
Mavrommatis Palestine Concessions case 31–32
MERCOSUR Protocols (1994) 76–77
  partnership *pro rata* claims 43, 45, 46–47
  transferability of claims and 38–39
  treaty obligation to protect all persons within jurisdiction and 39
nationality of corporation
  Barcelona Traction 40–41
    exceptions 41
  criteria/nexus 40
  Elettronica Sicula (ELSI) 41
  globalization and 42
  international registration and 42
  Iran–US Claims Tribunal 42–43
  ITLOS 81
  partnerships 43
  piercing the corporate veil 45–46
  shareholder rights and 40–41, 42
  state practice 41–42
nationality of ships, individual responsibility and 54
negotiation: *see* alternative dispute settlement procedures
Neville Brown, L. 99
New York Convention on the Recognition and Enforcement of Foreign Arbitral Awards (1958) 72–73, 111
NGOs
  advisory opinion, right to request 20–21, 59–60
  screening process, need for 60
  politicization of ICC and 57
  politicization of ICJ and 20–21, 59–60
  role 1–2
    participation in decision-making of international organizations 80
    professionalism, need for 81, 94–95
  standing
    ITLOS 82
    WTO Dispute Settlement Understanding (DSU) 93–94
non-state actors, role 1–2
Nørgaard, C. 29–30
Nürnberg Tribunal 54

OECD
  Multilateral Agreement on Investments (draft) (1998) 69–70
  developing countries and 69–70

152

Index

Index

Schneider, M.E. 44
Schoenbaum, T.J. 92, 93, 96–97
Schreuer, C. 65
Schwarzenberger, G. 11–12
Schwebel, S.M. 20, 21–22, 113, 121–122
Scott, J.B. 110
Seabed Disputes Chamber, jurisdiction: *see*
    International Tribunal for the Law of the
    Sea (ITLOS)
Security Council
  exclusivity of powers 24
  judicial review
    advisory jurisdiction and 26
    exclusion 25
    federal precedent, relevance 23–25
    ICJ/ICTY decisions as 24–26
    interpretation of Security Council decisions
      by UN bodies other than ICJ 26
    judicial development and application of
      principles of international law as 25–26
  legitimate self-defense 23
  "police state" role 15
  as public trust 15
  renewal/enhancement of role 22–23
  separation of powers concept, absence 24
  unauthorized action by member states 23
  ex post facto authorization, relevance 23
self-defense, legitimacy 23
self-regulation 118
separation of powers 24, 27, 126
Shihata, I.F.I. 63–64, 79–80 101, 102
Shihata, I.F.I. and Parra, A.R. 64–65, 66
Skubiszewski, K. 23–24
Sluiter, G. 55–56
small claims procedures 117–118
  Swiss Claims Resolution Tribunal (dormant
    accounts) 117–118
  UNCC 117–118
soft law 6
Sohn, L.B. 2, 20, 103–104, 110
Sohn, L.B. and Baxter, R.R. 37
South Africa, Truth and Reconciliation
    Commission 106
sovereign immunity
  erosion of doctrine 62
  individual's right of access to domestic court
    and 62
  remedy, inherent right to and 35–36
sovereignty: *see also* state as principal subject of
    international law
  developing countries 4

environment and 4
European Union 4
human rights and 4
selective limitation 7
  transfer of powers/competences to
    international organizations 7
Specht, P. 96
standing: *see* individual, standing before
    international tribunal
state immunity: *see* sovereign immunity
state practice
  continuity of nationality 36
  nationality of corporation 41–42
state as principal subject of international law
    1–2, 4, 5, 8, 125: *see also* sovereignty
  changing role 29–31
state responsibility for internationally wrongful
    acts 5–6
  diplomatic protection and 32
stateless persons, diplomatic protection
    35–36
Sullivan, D.S. 102
Suy, E. 11–12, 13–14
Switzerland, Claims Resolution Tribunal
    (dormant accounts) 117–118

technological developments 3–4
terrorism, self-defence, legitimacy 23
Tomuschat, C. 13–14, 17
Torres Bernárdez, S. 109–111, 112
trade cooperation 2
Trakman, L.E. 73
treaty interpretation
  Free Trade Commission (NAFTA), role 69
  ICJ, role 61
Trevor-Roper, H. and Urban, G. 3
Tridimas, T. 118
Truth and Reconciliation Commission
  Chile 106
  local traditions, respect for 106–107
  South Africa 106

UK (subsequently Canada)–US, Treaty Relating
    to Boundary Waters (1909) 108–9
UN Compensation Commission
  applicable law 44
  corporate claims
    Decision 123 (2001) (non-Kuwaiti
      nationals) 45–46
    direct application by corporation 45
    joint venture claims 45

154

Index